EMPLOYEE RIGHTS

IN MARYLAND

Gregg H. Mosson

EMPLOYEE RIGHTS
IN MARYLAND

A CONCISE GUIDE TO KNOWING AND
PROTECTING YOUR RIGHTS

Published by Advantage, Charleston, South Carolina.
Member of Advantage Media Group.

ADVANTAGE is a registered trademark, and the Advantage colophon is a trademark of Advantage Media Group, Inc.

Printed in the United States of America.

10 9 8 7 6 5 4 3 2 1

ISBN: 978-1-64225-347-4
LCCN: 2021916889

Book design by Mary Hamilton.

This publication is designed to provide accurate and authoritative information in regard to the subject matter covered. It is sold with the understanding that the publisher is not engaged in rendering legal, accounting, or other professional services. If legal advice or other expert assistance is required, the services of a competent professional person should be sought. This book does not constitute legal advice.

 Advantage Media Group is proud to be a part of the Tree Neutral® program. Tree Neutral offsets the number of trees consumed in the production and printing of this book by taking proactive steps such as planting trees in direct proportion to the number of trees used to print books. To learn more about Tree Neutral, please visit **www.treeneutral.com**.

Advantage Media Group is a publisher of business, self-improvement, and professional development books and online learning. We help entrepreneurs, business leaders, and professionals share their Stories, Passion, and Knowledge to help others Learn & Grow. Do you have a manuscript or book idea that you would like us to consider for publishing? Please visit **advantagefamily.com** or call **1.866.775.1696**.

Knowledge is power, knowledge is safety, knowledge is happiness.

—Thomas Jefferson
from a *Letter to George Tickner,*
November 25, 1817

Be the change you want to see in the world.

—attributed to Mahatma Gandhi

Please Take Notice

This guide is dedicated to providing an overview of employment law in Maryland, including at-will employment, contractual employment, and major federal and state laws shaping employment law and rights. *It is not exhaustive and not legal advice.* For legal advice, seek a lawyer. In keeping with Mr. Jefferson, this guide aims to make each and every reader more knowledgeable, and so more effective in their lives and careers.

CONTENTS

INTRODUCTION

Are you working in Maryland and either running into roadblocks or seeking greater knowledge about employee rights? If so, this guide offers practical information to help you protect your workplace rights and working career. The perfect time to read it is when you begin working in Maryland. The essential time to read it is when you have a problem.

The guide covers various employee rights in Maryland. However, it is not a comprehensive legal resource. To be comprehensive would require thousands of pages, and even then some topics would be left out. It does, however, cover the basics, and it provides a list of references at the end for follow-up, giving you the opportunity to broaden the scope of your knowledge.

If you need to take an employment problem to court, however, you should find an experienced employment attorney. Why? Employment law is complex and rooted in a history of court precedent, as well as local, state, and federal statutory law. Without professional expertise in the law, you are vulnerable. Consequently, I also include a chapter about hiring a lawyer. However, maybe that is not your route. So I also include brief chapters on gathering and preserving evidence and using discovery at court.

I have handled hundreds of employment disputes at the various levels at which they occur, such as applying for medical leave, helping employees handle disputes at work themselves through HR or their union, negotiating with employers' counsel, and representing employees before governmental agencies and, of course, at state and federal court. Negotiating employment disputes can be frustrating, and knowing what carrots and sticks to wield requires finesse.

In addition, during my own career, I myself have navigated at-will, term, and contractual employment, as well as entrepreneurship. So I bring real-world experience to understand employment problems. Overall, this guide compiles my experience handling at-will, contractual, and unionized employment in a way that I think is helpful and broadly applicable.

The first step in tackling any problem is knowing your rights and options, so let's get started!

USING THIS GUIDE

A s stated in the introduction, this guide offers a general overview of the landscape of employment rights under state and federal law in Maryland. Consider it an aerial map. It does not include every nook and cranny of the land, but it does cover the basics: at-will employment, the employee handbook, owed wages, union matters, illegal workplace discrimination and retaliation, leave from work laws, unemployment benefits, and workers' compensation. It also covers evidence, court discovery, and seeking legal advice, among other topics.

Importantly, I must repeat that this book does not constitute legal advice and tell you a little more about why. Books about specific areas of employment law, such as the US Fair Labor Standards Act (FLSA) or the US Americans with Disabilities Act (ADA), each comprise around a thousand pages or more. This guide, on the other hand, is succinct and written with an eye toward knowing, protecting, and asserting employee rights. Further, legal advice is tailored to each person's particular situation. However, this guide is for a general audience. For example, in an employment dispute, a legal analyst might need to know the following:

- any mistakes alleged

- the facts in dispute

- the facts agreed upon

- when the matter in question happened

- who was there (witnesses)

- who are the main players

- what was said

- what was placed in writing

- the surrounding chain of events

- any relevant employment contract, handbook, grievance procedure, and/or policy document

- further circumstances specific to the matter at hand

In other words, legal advice applies specifically while this guide applies generally. Further, the law changes, whether annually through the Maryland legislature, periodically through the federal government, or whenever a new court decision or government agency regulation arises. So, again, if you need legal advice, please seek it from an attorney.

CHAPTER ONE

THE WORLD OF AT-WILL EMPLOYMENT

WHAT IS AT-WILL EMPLOYMENT?

I suggest you think of at-will employment as a party, because, like a party, it involves social ties, can be enjoyable or a downer, and lacks a guarantee. Here are some questions that often apply to both parties and at-will employment:

- Are you invited?

- Has the schedule changed?

- Has the engagement been canceled?

- Does someone want you disinvited?

- Do you still want to go?

Let's stick with this party analogy for a second. If you show up on Friday night and the party's canceled, but your friend forgot to tell you, can you sue the host? Mostly likely not. You'll need to take your personal party elsewhere.

But hey, it works both ways. If you yourself fail to show up and the guests have less fun as a result, the host cannot sue you either because you have a right to stay home or attend a better party. Similarly, in the world of at-will employment, you have the right to quit and move on.

LET'S DISCUSS AT-WILL EMPLOYMENT

The term "at-will" employment covers most employment where there is no written contract, including no union contract, and often assumes the lack of protection under governmental civil service rules.

New public school teachers, for example, may be on written annual term contracts that have renewal clauses. Teachers and/or other craft professionals also may have union contracts that govern their workplaces in terms of performance, transfer to another workplace, pay scales, imposition of discipline, and the like.

In Maryland, unless you have a written employment contract, you are most likely an at-will employee. If someone promises verbally that you will have a job for a period of time (a "term"), that promise can be considered part of an employment agreement or oral contract. However, such a promise will be very difficult to prove unless your employer admits it because Maryland law will presume no such promise unless it is in writing. Instead, Maryland law presumes an at-will employment relationship (see Bontempo v. Lare, 444 Md. 344, 364-65, 119 A.3d 791, 803-04 (2015)).

IN MARYLAND, UNLESS YOU HAVE A WRITTEN EMPLOYMENT CONTRACT, YOU ARE MOST LIKELY AN AT-WILL EMPLOYEE.

By definition, at-will employment means that neither employer nor employee needs a reason to end the employment. Consequently, employers may, and often do, end such employment due to alleged poor performance or for "business reasons," such as loss of revenue and/or changing circumstances. Likewise, employees may, and often do, quit, either because they have better job offers or simply because they do not wish to continue. While these are typical motivations for termination of employment, however, the legal doctrine of at-will employment does not require a reason for termination. Nor does it require either side to disclose why they are parting ways.

LIMITATIONS UPON AT-WILL EMPLOYMENT

At-will employment, which arose to dominance in the nineteenth century in America with the expansion of factories and industrial production, has twenty-first century limitations. Two primary sources of these limitations are private contract and statutory law. For instance, state and federal laws prohibit certain discriminatory and/or retaliatory motives as reasons to take employment actions, including firing someone. Some examples are discussed in chapter 10.

Limitations to at-will employment, however, include more than discriminatory and/or retaliatory motives. A patchwork of intersecting laws constitutes a set of restrictions to the doctrine of at-will employment, some of which are covered in chapters 3, 8-11, and 13.

Business owners, for instance, cannot legally fire employees because they request medical leave under the

US Family Medical Leave Act (FMLA) and so inconvenience the staff. Such a violation of law, if proven true, likely will be deemed "illegal FMLA interference" if it happens in advance of the medical leave, or "illegal FMLA retaliation" if it happens afterward.

NOTICE AND GRIEVANCE PROVISIONS

Notice and grievance provisions within an employment or union contract may alter the at-will employment relationship. A notice provision, for instance, may require a set time like two weeks or thirty days of notice in advance before either side can end the employment. If so, these notice provisions should be in writing, because the customary "two weeks' notice" is just that, customary, in the context of at-will employment, where none is required by law.

A grievance procedure also may change the structure of how employment is handled, if it exists, and likewise should be in writing. This guide has specific sections in chapters 2, 4, and 5 on the employee handbook, union contracts, and grievance procedures that cover this and how it impacts the at-will employment relationship.

PROTECTING YOURSELF IN AN AT-WILL EMPLOYMENT RELATIONSHIP

How do you protect yourself in an at-will employment relationship? The following is a list of eight to-dos:

- First, have savings.

- Second, continually develop new skills for which there is high demand.

- Third, try hard in your current place of employment—but always develop your network and career at the same time.

- Fourth, if there are problems at work, look for another position while you still have a job, as employers will find you more attractive if you're already employed. Further, sometimes personality conflicts at work, if that is the irksome snafu, cannot be resolved.

- Fifth, if laid off, consider self- or part-time employment. This will improve your skills and reputation.

- Sixth, if let go, file for unemployment benefits.

- Seventh, if possible, work in a field that offers union or professional employment contracts.

- Eighth, if an employee, obtain and read your employee handbook, which, as discussed in chapter 2, is a guide to your employer's policies and point of view.

CONCLUSION

As noted, at-will employment is analogous to a party in an important way—the lack of a guarantee. Further, it's no fun if you have to litigate an employment claim rather than focus on income or career. So, as discussed throughout this guide, learning what your employment rights are is prudent. Knowledge is power; therefore, the next chapter discusses obtaining and reading your employment handbook as a preventative measure—your first basic step to self-protection.

> **AT-WILL EMPLOYMENT IS ANALOGOUS TO A PARTY IN AN IMPORTANT WAY–THE LACK OF A GUARANTEE**.

CHAPTER TWO

THE EMPLOYEE HANDBOOK

A Good Negotiation Tool

I n the world of at-will employment, the employee handbook provides you with knowledge and options about what to do, where to go, and whom to speak to as available in your specific workplace, at least according to the employer's written policies. As part of strategic routine onboarding, you should, therefore, obtain and read your employee handbook. Yet, in my experience, few do—until, of course, they need to.

WHAT IS IN THE EMPLOYEE HANDBOOK?

An employer's handbook, which is often called "the employee handbook" at work, usually describes policies regarding many aspects of working life and procedures, including the following:

- employment benefits, including insurance options, holiday pay, and other paid benefits like tuition benefits

- an outline of the employer's disciplinary policy

- a "hotline" number for workplace problems such as discrimination

- an explanation of any "grievance procedure" used to air grievances to someone besides your direct supervisor

- what kinds of "leave" are available (including leave provided by the employer, rather than simply mandated by law)

Any Maryland employee handbook also likely addresses whether accrued benefit pay (like sick and vacation pay accrued but not yet used) is forfeited or paid out when the job ends—a matter discussed later in this chapter.

Let's take a look at some of these features of the employee handbook.

The Progressive Discipline Policy

Many employee handbooks include a discipline or "progressive discipline" policy. Such a policy can be a good negotiation tool. However, discipline policies often are not enforceable under law because of a handbook disclaimer provision, discussed further below. If not legally enforceable, this means that employers often have the legal right to choose whether and how to use them.

If facing a difficult supervisor, sometimes knowing the employer's policy will help you better communicate with that person, or at least diplomatically justify your own conduct at work. Meanwhile, you might consider dusting off your résumé.

You should also, however, be aware that in illegal discrimination, retaliation, and whistleblowing cases, among other types of lawsuits, if the progressive discipline policy is skipped or falsified, this can be used as evidence of illegal motive. In such a situation, while the policies themselves remain nonenforceable, their use or lack thereof can constitute evidence of a hidden illegal motive, as is discussed in chapter 10 on discrimination.

The Disclaimer

The employee handbook usually does not change the nature of at-will employment. This is because most have a "clear and conspicuous disclaimer" to protect the at-will nature of the employment relationship. The exact wording of such disclaimers can differ; however, many are written something like the following:

> **THE EMPLOYEE HANDBOOK USUALLY DOES NOT CHANGE THE NATURE OF AT-WILL EMPLOYMENT.**

> THIS COMPANY IS AN AT-WILL EMPLOYER. THIS MEANS THAT REGARDLESS OF ANY PROVISION IN THIS EMPLOYEE HANDBOOK, THE COMPANY OR I MAY TERMINATE THE EMPLOYMENT RELATIONSHIP AT ANY TIME, FOR ANY REASON, WITH OR WITHOUT CAUSE OR NOTICE. NOTHING IN THIS EMPLOYEE HANDBOOK OR IN ANY DOCUMENT OR STATEMENT, WRITTEN OR ORAL, SHALL LIMIT THE RIGHT TO TERMINATE EMPLOYMENT AT-WILL.

If the disclaimer is conspicuous and clear, Maryland law will honor the fact that it is up to the employer whether and how to use these policies. Consequently, if such a disclaimer is in the handbook, the handbook has no force of law against the employer (see, e.g., Castiglione v. Johns Hopkins Hosp., 69 Md. App. 325, 517 A.2d 786 (1986)). A disclaimer at the beginning of the handbook reasonably can be seen by Maryland courts as applying to the entire handbook (see Elliott v. Bd. of Trs., 104 Md. App. 93, 100-06, 655 A.2d 46, 49-52 (1995)).

There are rare exceptions to this. If the disclaimer is not clear and conspicuous—for instance, if the employer has separated some sections from the handbook onto a website and not reprinted the disclaimer online—those separate sections might be enforceable (see Tucker v. Johns Hopkins Univ., No. 1150 (Md. Ct. Spec. App. Apr. 10, 2017), unreported opinion).

In Tucker, the court solely held that an employee, Mr. Tucker, had a right to a three-person panel review of his firing by Johns Hopkins, but he could not use the court process to change the outcome of his firing simply because the process was inadequate. In other words, the court held that Johns Hopkins was legally required to honor their own website's promise of this three-person panel review procedure. Yet, if the organization wanted to rubber-stamp the termination via the panel procedure, the court would not examine it. The

Tucker case provides a process right and nothing more, and it is a good example of the limits of mere procedural rights within the at-will employment relationship.

In Elliott v. Bd. of Trs., supra, the Maryland Court of Special Appeals notes that employer promises made in documents without disclaimers, or simply made separately from the typical employee handbook containing a legal disclaimer, can become part of the employment benefit bargained for by working for the employer, or simply continuing to do so, if facts so justify.

Owed Benefits at End of Employment

In Maryland, an employer must pay out to the employee any accrued sick time, vacation, or personal pay—unless the employee handbook or other written policy states otherwise. If the employer's written policy is silent on this matter, these benefits must be paid out (see Maryland Wage Payment and Collection Law, Md. Code, Lab. & Empl. § 3-505(b) (2021)). So this issue first is decided by looking at the employee handbook and employer's written policies.

However, not every employer provides these benefits or provides all of them. This all being said, check your handbook and see what it says. Know your rights.

At-Will Requests to Reconsider

I have entitled this section "At-Will Requests to Reconsider" because some large employers in Maryland voluntarily provide an appeal procedure to enable terminated or disciplined at-will employees to appeal, even though, as at-will employees, they don't have any legal right to ensure some decision is reversed or some facts are investigated. For example, a request to reconsider may enable at-will employees to appeal a termination, suspension, or demotion to persons outside their daily milieu. It may enable them to reduce some discipline imposed, obtain a transfer of work station, or be offered a second chance.

However, because such procedures lack force of law, as in the Tucker case just discussed, this reconsideration procedure usually is not enforceable. In other words, it is an opportunity to persuade but not to force the employer to change a decision. In sum, requests to reconsider often permit obtaining a review of what happened beyond the purview of your immediate supervisor, which can be helpful.

In my experience, these procedures require that any written request to reconsider be filed within five to fifteen days of the problematic event at issue (often at the quicker end of this spectrum). This being said, the time allotted depends on the employer's procedure, which is often in writing, such as in the employer's handbook, HR department's files, or online. Obtain it. A request to reconsider, for instance, may require you, as a first step, to present a written request to the same supervisor who took the problematic action. While doing so might seem futile, skipping it could result in the appeal's denial on the basis of incorrect procedure.

Again, even if legally unenforceable, these procedures can be helpful, especially when used respectfully, strategically, and tactfully to achieve some solution, including correction of mistakes.

READING YOUR HANDBOOK

These days, your employee handbook may be online. If you click a button affirming that you received it but you do not actually read it, or at least ask for a hard copy to read later, a court likely will nonetheless deem you informed (or, as the courts sometimes say, "noticed"). As courts generally frown upon persons who affirm one thing and then seek to retract it during a lawsuit, a person facing some problem at work who claims not to know about a "hotline" in the handbook or other remedy will face an uphill battle if it becomes an important fact about whether they knew or not. If that same employee affirmed, some years earlier during the busy work day, to have read an employee handbook alerting them to this same hotline or other remedial process, then they may be held to it later at court. I have dealt with this problem, and the reality is that sometimes it cannot be legally repaired.

CONCLUSION

KNOWLEDGE IS POWER, SO KNOW YOUR EMPLOYEE HANDBOOK.

Possessing and reading your employee handbook gives you a basis for dialogue, knowledge of your employer's rules and policies, and provides a valuable negotiation tool. Knowledge is power, so know your employee handbook.

CHAPTER THREE

WAGE RIGHTS AND OWED WAGES

You have a right to be paid for the work that you do. Guess what: Maryland law can help too. The Maryland Wage Payment and Collection Law (MWPCL) helps employees seek owed pay and also structures how to pay employees in Maryland (Md. Code, Lab. & Empl., § 3-501 et seq. (2021)).

The MWPCL, for example, defines "wages" very broadly to

YOU HAVE A RIGHT TO BE PAID FOR THE WORK THAT YOU DO. GUESS WHAT: MARYLAND LAW CAN HELP TOO.

cover any wage or salary, overtime, any bonus or commission owed, and "any other remuneration promised for service" (*Id.* § 3-501(c)(2)).

Employers face penalties for violating the MWPCL, which helps encourage compliance. Under the MWPCL, judges have the discretion to award wronged employees up to three total times the amount owed—as well as any legal costs—if the employer is wrong and especially if willfully so (MWPCL § 3-507(b)(1)).

In other words, as the following quote details, if your employer owes you $5,000 and you sue and prove it, the court has the discretion to award you an additional $10,000 to total "treble damages" (three times total what's owed):

> IF, IN AN ACTION UNDER SUBSECTION (A) OF THIS SECTION, A COURT FINDS THAT AN EMPLOYER WITHHELD THE WAGE OF AN EMPLOYEE IN VIOLATION OF THIS SUBTITLE AND NOT AS A RESULT OF A BONA FIDE DISPUTE, THE COURT MAY AWARD THE EMPLOYEE AN AMOUNT NOT EXCEEDING 3 TIMES THE WAGE, AND REASONABLE COUNSEL FEES AND OTHER COSTS. (MWPCL § 3-507(B)(1))

As the Maryland Court of Appeals, the state's highest court, explained in detail, a court is encouraged to award legal expenses in addition to whatever pay is owed so as to ensure that the employee is made whole when an employer wrongfully withholds wages (see Peters v. Early Healthcare Giver, Inc., 439 Md. 646 (2014); see also Skripchenko v. VIRxSYS Corp., Civ. No. TDC-13-0004, 2014 US Dist. LEXIS 136423, at *31-33 (D. Md. Sep. 26, 2014)—endorsing awarding legal expenses as part of the law's remedial purpose).

Again, as noted above, an award of these penalty damages depends upon proving willful wrongdoing, compared to there being a "bona fide" dispute over the amount owed, whether it is owed or not, or other legitimate concern preventing payment. A bona fide dispute involves a legitimate basis, including a reasonable mistake in good faith. Further, if the court thinks the matter simply was not egregious, it has the discretion to decline to impose some or all of penalty damages (see Peters, supra). Some tips for taking an employer to court are discussed later in this chapter.

DEMANDING OWED PAY

If you are working without being paid, you should consider doing four things immediately:

- First, make a written record of the time you work and are not paid.

- Second, look for better employment.

- Third, if you speak to coworkers or supervisors about working without pay, make notes in which you include the date, time, names of persons with whom you spoke, and what was said.

- Fourth, consider making a written demand that you be paid. Of course, if you still work for the employer, this may be tricky. So, practically speaking, it may be easier to do so once you have another job lined up.

Making a demand can help get you paid. First, if an employer receives a written demand for owed wages or payment for working off the clock, it will be difficult for that employer to argue later that any nonpayment was a bona fide mistake or in dispute, because your written demand may become evidence of willful wage theft. Second, employers count on the intimidation, and sometimes desperation, of their workforce to avoid paying. However, they may also fear a potential investigation or court entanglement and so give in once they know an employee is serious about being paid. Additionally, sometimes refusal to pay occurs on a supervisory level, and a written demand may force a course correction within a company. Consequently, for these reasons, a written demand is useful to avoid court through resolution, and at court if not.

YOU CAN'T SIGN AWAY PAY

Lastly, MWPCL § 3-502(f) holds that an employee cannot waive his or her right to agreed-upon wages for work performed. An employee cannot simply sign some document and forfeit their pay. Maryland law includes a strong anti-waiver provision to protect employees from such pressure (*Id.*; Cunningham v. Feinberg, 441 Md. 310, 344-48, 107 A.3d 1194, 1215-18 (2015), discussing).

COMPLAINING TO THE MARYLAND DEPARTMENT OF LABOR

The Maryland Department of Labor advises people seeking their wages to demand what is owed in writing via US Certified Mail, Return Receipt Requested (which is that green card coming back to you). The US Postal Service can explain how to do this.

Such demands should provide details about the work performed and monies owed, for instance, the dates and hours of the work performed, the rate of the pay agreed to, and the total demanded. Keep a copy of the letter, and when you receive the green card back, save that too. Then wait thirty days. Sometimes, as mentioned above, the employer will pay because they do not want to be subject to a lawsuit or penalty damages. However, once thirty days has expired without answer, you can make a complaint to the Maryland Department of Labor (providing you have the aforementioned proof of your demand).

Maryland law authorizes the Maryland Department of Labor to present your demand for pay to the employer as well as to help enforce this payment through various lawful means (see MWPCL § 3-507, 3-507.1). In other words, the state may help you.

SEEKING PENALTY PAY AT COURT

As discussed, Maryland law provides penalty damages to deter employers from refusing to pay without reason (see Skripchenko v. VIRxSYS Corp., supra; accord MWPCL § 3-507.2(b)). Therefore, if you have issued a well-written and clear demand for payment by letter or email and the employer has ignored it or refused payment, a court may find this the willful wrong necessary to provide penalty pay. Such a "refusal to comply" is evidence of willful bad faith and therefore justifies penalty pay (see Cruz v. Home & Garden Concepts, LLC, Civ. No. GJH-15-204, 2016 US Dist. LEXIS 89880, at *16-18 (D. Md. July 12, 2016)).

Further, a lack of "due diligence" (meaning that your employer ignored your demand without explanation) prevents an employer from claiming a good-faith mistake at court and therefore justifies penalty damages (see Pinnacle Grp., LLC v. Kelly, 235 Md. App. 436, 448-50 & 453-55, 178 A.3d 581, 589-90 & 592-93 (2018)).

In contrast, a good-faith attempt at fair resolution addresses the employer's burden to show there was a bona fide disagreement (rather than blunt refusal to pay) and avoid these penalties, even if payment is held to be due and owed (see Macsherry v. Sparrows Point, LLC, Civ. No. ELH-15-22, 2017 US Dist. LEXIS 122153, at *83-86 (D. Md. Aug. 3, 2017)).

HOW MWPCL STRUCTURES PAY

The MWPCL helps employees only, not self-employed people, to get paid. It does not help independent contractors because independent contractors do not possess an "employee right" under the MWPCL. The MWPCL helps employees collect their "wages," a term defined as "all compensation that is due to an employee for employment" (§ 3-501(c)(1)). However, if you are an independent business person or independent contractor, you likely have other kinds of payment rights (not addressed here), especially under Maryland contract law.

The MWPCL also requires employers to pay employees in regular pay periods, typically twice per month. "Administrative, executive, or professional employee(s)" may be paid less frequently, but must still be paid regularly (§ 3-502(a)).

While normal tax and other standard deductions from pay are permissible, an employer seeking to withhold pay for some reason (such as, for example, damage to a work vehicle) cannot lawfully deduct from pay unless "authorized expressly in writing by the employee" (§ 3-503(2)). In Maryland, a fired employee must be paid out his or her last check that falls on the next pay period after the termination date (§ 3-505(a)).

Whether accrued leave pay also is paid out when an employee quits or is terminated depends on the employer's handbook or written policy (§ 3-505(b)). If the employer's policy provides clear written rules and the employer provides you with a copy, then the written rules govern. If, however, the handbook or other written policy notice does not specify, the accrued leave and accrued benefit pay must be paid out (§ 3-505(b)).

MINIMUM WAGE AND OVERTIME

The rights to be paid the minimum wage, overtime, or a salary are codified in both Maryland and federal law, under the Maryland Wage and Hour Law (Md. Code, Lab. & Empl § 3-401 et seq. (MWHL)), and the US Fair Labor Standards Act of 1938 (29 U.S.C. § 201 et seq. (FLSA)). However, these laws do not apply to all types of employees (excepting certain professionals and executives, among others). Exploring exceptions is beyond this guide's scope, however. Further, the remainder of this chapter cites mostly Maryland law.

Where applicable, both federal and Maryland laws guarantee a minimum wage (see MWHL, § 3-428(b)(1)(i)). Likewise, both guarantee overtime, which is 1.5 times your pay for time over forty hours per week worked, where it is applicable (see MWHL, § 3-415(a)).

If a wage dispute goes to court and is decided in the employee's favor, the court is instructed to award the employee what is owed plus an additional equal sum, to double it, under a penalty provision called "liquidated damages." The law also instructs a court to have the employer cover the reasonable legal fees and costs of the employee in bringing suit (MWHL, § 3-427(d)(1)).

EMPLOYER'S DUTY TO KEEP RECORDS VERSUS WORKING OFF THE CLOCK

In Maryland, an employer has a responsibility to keep records of the daily and weekly hours employees work and to keep them for three years after the work is performed (Md. Code Ann., Lab. & Empl. § 3-424). This is true under the federal law as well, where it applies (see Dept. of Labor Reg. 29 C.F.R. § 1620.32).

This law becomes important if you are seeking owed pay and the employer claims to have no records of your work. That's because if you yourself have kept good records, a court can rely on them to award you pay, thereby preventing employers from shirking their legal duty with the "nobody knows" defense (see Marroquin v. Canales, 505 F. Supp. 2d 283, 295-98 (D. Md. 2007) (construing Maryland law); Martin v. Deiriggi, Civ. No. 88-0064-C(K), 1991 US Dist. LEXIS 22063, at *27 (N.D.W. Va. Dec. 12, 1991)— "this burden on the defendants is a heavy one, because otherwise they would benefit from having violated the record-keeping requirements of the Act"—construing federal law).

KEEPING RECORDS YOURSELF

There are several ways to create written records of unpaid time, and concerning other workplace matters.

You can keep a journal of dates and hours worked, for instance, whether on your phone, in a notepad you keep in your car, or at home. If being cheated of pay due to working off the clock, you should keep these records at the end of every shift. Plus, after a while, events blur, but a written record remains accurate.

AFTER A WHILE, EVENTS BLUR, BUT A WRITTEN RECORD REMAINS ACCURATE.

NO RETALIATION ALLOWED

Both US and Maryland law protect workers who are fired, demoted, or otherwise seriously punished after demanding their owed minimum wage and/or overtime. Such punishment is called "retaliation," and it is illegal (MWHL, § 3-428(b)(1)(iii) & (b)(2); FLSA, 29. U.S.C. § 215(a)).

A NOTE ON INDEPENDENT CONTRACTORS

Independent contractors who are owed money are owed under the terms of a written contract or oral agreement. This type of work relationship falls under Maryland contract law. However, employers who misclassify "employees" as independent contractors cannot escape the aforementioned wage and pay laws merely by doing so. Courts routinely approach misclassification cases by examining the facts over labels. Such misclassification cases are complicated. If you are in such a situation, seek an attorney's advice to determine whether you are an independent contractor or an employee under US and Maryland law.

CONCLUSION

In Maryland, employees are entitled to be paid what they are owed, and employers face penalties for violating wage right laws. However, in a dispute over pay, it is nonetheless prudent to document your work, any violations of law, demands for payment and to know the legal remedies available. Remember, knowledge is power, so know your rights.

CHAPTER FOUR

UNION CONTRACTS AND THE NATIONAL LABOR RELATIONS ACT

U nions arose over a century ago because at-will employment provides zero job protection. However, today, American culture seems largely opposed to unions. This is due to a combination of factors: stagnant wage growth and low wages that strain the affordability of union dues, union leaders in the private sector losing more fights in recent decades than winning, the negative image of union mobsters in movies, and union representatives who are not always effective.

UNION CONTRACTS

Whatever their flaws, unions nonetheless provide members with a union contract. This contract is governed by the US National Labor Relations Act (NLRA), 29 U.S.C. § 151-169. If you are a union member, you should obtain and read a copy. The contract provides you with legal rights.

For-Cause Protection

The standard right in any union contract is that you can be disciplined and terminated only "for cause," or, in other words, for a valid reason. Unlike with at-will employment, a union's "for cause" clause provides legal protection from an arbitrary employment action. First, as noted, it requires that the employer act based upon a reason. Second, if an employee challenges an action, the employer usually must provide that reason, and third, defend it.

Let me give you an example of how powerful a right to for-cause protection can be. In my practice, I have received several calls from supervisors and employees who say they stopped a workplace fight but were subsequently fired for fighting. In an at-will employment context, the employer has no legal obligation to investigate it. The employer can fire the employee either for fighting or simply so as to move on from the incident. This is because at-will employees have no guaranteed right to work. So even if there is a reason, there's certainly no legal obligation to prove it's real, valid, based on fact, or inappropriate. It simply doesn't matter—at least not legally. In contrast, in contractual employment with for-cause protection, if a coworker stops a fight, yet is accused of fighting and is fired, he or she has a right to challenge this accusation and potentially correct the matter.

Filing a Grievance

Union contracts almost certainly include a grievance procedure, which usually is the mechanism for challenging issues affecting employment. The grievance procedure, for instance, often can be used to challenge a for-cause termination. How powerful it is depends in part on the power of the union that bargained for it and the specific written procedure.

I discuss the grievance procedure more fully in chapter 5.

FILING A LABOR CHARGE

As noted above, unions exist under the NLRA. The act is enforced by the National Labor Relations Board

(NLRB), which has a regional investigatory office for each state. The Maryland office is in Baltimore, Maryland. As of 2021, you can contact the office at:

NLRB, REGION 5 OFFICE

100 S. CHARLES ST., SUITE 600

BALTIMORE, MD 21202

TEL: (410) 962-2822

FAX: (410) 962-2198

You also can access the NLRB website at www. nlrb.gov (nationally) and https://www.nlrb.gov/ about-nlrb/who-we-are/regional-offices/region-05-baltimore (Maryland) to find further helpful resources for navigating union-based employment or about forming a union.

Importantly, you have a right to file a charge against your employer if the employer is busting your union or otherwise harms your rights protected by the act. You also have a right to file a charge against your union for failure of representation. A charge of an unfair labor practice must be filed within six months of the occurrence (29 US Code § 160(b)).

Finally, you have an opportunity to consult with the NLRB about employment practices, such as what is normal and what is illegal.

FORM NLRB-501 (2-18)	UNITED STATES OF AMERICA NATIONAL LABOR RELATIONS BOARD CHARGE AGAINST EMPLOYER	DO NOT WRITE IN THIS SPACE	
		Case	Date Filed

INSTRUCTIONS:
File an original with NLRB Regional Director for the region in which the alleged unfair labor practice occurred or is occurring.

1. EMPLOYER AGAINST WHOM CHARGE IS BROUGHT

a. Name of Employer	b. Tel. No.
	c. Cell No.
	f. Fax. No.
d. Address *(Street, city, state, and ZIP code)* e. Employer Representative	g. e-mail
	h. Number of workers employed
i. Type of Establishment *(factory, mine, wholesaler, etc.)* j. Identify principal product or service	

The above-named employer has engaged in and is engaging in unfair labor practices within the meaning of section 8(a), subsections (1) and
(list subsections) _____ of the National Labor Relations Act, and these unfair labor
practices are practices affecting commerce within the meaning of the Act, or these unfair labor practices affecting commerce within the meaning of
the Act and the Postal Reorganization Act.

2. Basis of the Charge *(set forth a clear and concise statement of the facts constituting the alleged unfair labor practices)*

SAMPLE ONLY / ILLUSTRATIVE PURPOSE

3. Full name of party filing charge *(if labor organization, give full name, including local name and number)*

4a. Address *(Street and number, city, state, and ZIP code)*	4b. Tel. No.
	4c. Cell No.
	4d. Fax No.
	4e. e-mail

5. Full name of national or international labor organization of which it is an affiliate or constituent unit *(to be filled in when charge is filed by a labor organization)*

6. DECLARATION
I declare that I have read the above charge and that the statements are true to the best of my knowledge and belief.

		Tel. No.
(signature of representative or person making charge) _(Print/type name and title or office, if any)_		Office, if any, Cell No.
		Fax No.
Address _____ Date _____		e-mail

WILLFUL FALSE STATEMENTS ON THIS CHARGE CAN BE PUNISHED BY FINE AND IMPRISONMENT (U.S. CODE, TITLE 18, SECTION 1001)

PRIVACY ACT STATEMENT
Solicitation of the information on this form is authorized by the National Labor Relations Act (NLRA), 29 U.S.C. § 151 et seq. The principal use of the information is to assist the National Labor Relations Board (NLRB) in processing unfair labor practice and related proceedings or litigation. The routine uses for the information are fully set forth in the Federal Register, 71 Fed. Reg. 74942-43 (Dec. 13, 2006). The NLRB will further explain these uses upon request. Disclosure of this information to the NLRB is voluntary; however, failure to supply the information may cause the NLRB to decline to invoke its processes.

6. DECLARATION
I declare that I have read the above charge and that the statements are true to the best of my knowledge and belief.

(signature of representative or person making charge)   _(Print/type name and title or office, if any)_

Address _____   Date _____

NLRB Charge against employer

RIGHT TO CONCERTED ACTIVITY AND TO DISCUSS PAY

Section 7 of the NLRA, applied to all employers engaged in interstate commerce, provides protection for two or more coworkers who discuss important working conditions or act in concert to improve them. Without doubt, pay and safety are two matters accepted as important to any job, so discussion of them by coworkers is protected by the act. The act's section 7 is quoted below:

> *EMPLOYEES SHALL HAVE THE RIGHT* TO SELF-ORGANIZATION, TO FORM, JOIN, OR ASSIST LABOR ORGANIZA-TIONS, TO BARGAIN COLLECTIVELY THROUGH REPRESENTATIVES OF THEIR OWN CHOOSING, AND *TO ENGAGE IN OTHER CONCERTED ACTIVITIES FOR THE PURPOSE OF* COLLECTIVE BAR-GAINING OR *OTHER MUTUAL AID* OR *PROTECTION,* AND SHALL ALSO HAVE THE RIGHT TO REFRAIN FROM ANY OR ALL OF SUCH ACTIVITIES EXCEPT TO THE EXTENT THAT SUCH RIGHT MAY BE AFFECTED BY AN AGREEMENT REQUIRING MEMBERSHIP IN A LABOR

ORGANIZATION AS A CONDITION OF EMPLOYMENT AS AUTHORIZED IN SECTION 158(A)(3) OF THIS TITLE. (29 US CODE § 157, EMPHASIS ADDED)

This section also provides a legal right to unionize, discuss unions, and try to create a union at work, or to assist a union. I have not highlighted that aspect, however, because I am focusing on the broader right, which protects employees who "engage" with one or more coworkers in "concerted activities" together for "mutual aid or protection."

This guide cannot go into detail about the legal definitions of concerted activity for mutual aid and protection. Let me say, though, that it must involve important (versus trivial) terms and conditions of one's work. Importantly, it also requires concerted activity, in other words, activity undertaken with someone else. You cannot stand alone and be protected by section 7.

WITHOUT DOUBT, PAY AND SAFETY ARE TWO MATTERS ACCEPTED AS IMPORTANT TO ANY JOB, SO DISCUSSION OF THEM BY COWORKERS IS PROTECTED BY THE ACT.

Under the NLRA, an employee has a right to speak with coworkers about pay (29 US Code § 157). Employers often frown on this, and for some cultural reason, in a competitive free-market economy, we often abide by an unspoken custom not to discuss our pay. However, we have a right to discuss it.

NLRA APPLIES TO PRIVATE BUSINESS IN INTERSTATE COMMERCE

The NLRA applies more broadly to the American workplace than simply authorizing unions. As discussed, it also applies, through the US Constitution's Interstate Commerce Clause, to businesses that engage in interstate commerce or affect interstate commerce.

However, the act's definition of interstate commerce has limits. It does not apply to every type of business handling goods that cross state borders. Instead, it often pertains only to businesses with $50,000 to $500,000 or more in annual revenue (depending on the industry). Because the threshold number depends on the industry, you have to check.

Further, the act does not apply to federal, state, or local government employees or to railroad employees. Maryland state employees have union rights and the right to engage "in other concerted activities for the purpose of collective bargaining or other mutual aid or protection" under Maryland law. Yet there are some additional limits, such as a ban on strikes (Md. Code, Ann., St. Gov. §§ 3-301, 3-303 (2021)).

Federal governmental employees derive their right to concerted activity from specific federal law and have significant civil service protections through the US Merit Systems Protections Board. Railroad employees are covered by the US Railway Labor Act of 1926 (see NLRA, 29 US Code § 152(2)).

CONCLUSION

Despite unions' flaws, union contractual protections should not be underestimated. The rights to know, inspect, and possibly challenge an employer's rationale for imposing termination or other workplace discipline is valuable. Consequently, if you are a union member, you should obtain and read your union contract, grievance procedure,

DESPITE UNIONS' FLAWS, UNION CONTRACTUAL PROTECTIONS SHOULD NOT BE UNDERESTIMATED.

and any grievance form available. Remember, knowledge is power, so know your workplace rights.

CHAPTER FIVE

FILING A GRIEVANCE

(If You Have a Grievance Process)

As previously discussed, a grievance procedure is a process, often a step-by-step one, that permits you to challenge a decision made against you. It often enables you to challenge a demotion, counseling memo, suspension from work, and/or termination. It also may enable you to challenge less drastic events, such as a worksite change, schedule change, and/or denial of a raise or benefit, depending on the grievance procedure involved. Grievance procedures are often found in union contracts, among civil service rules for various governmental workers, and sometimes in the private sector, too, as discussed both in chapter 2 and below.

In the context of unionized employment or other contract or civil service rules, grievance procedures carry the force of law because the law can be sought to aid in their enforcement. Sometimes union contracts define both what is included within and excluded from the grievance procedure. For instance, in one case I handled in 2020, a public sector teacher's contract did not permit "performance improvement plans" to be grieved but did permit a separate appeal process for these sorts of ongoing matters. The point is that grievance procedures often are highly specific and mandate precise procedures in writing that must be followed to appeal, grieve, or otherwise assert related legal rights.

AT-WILL REQUESTS TO RECONSIDER STILL CAN BE USEFUL IN EXPLORING NEGOTIATION OR REVISION OF SOME DECISION IF USED DIPLOMATICALLY.

Grievance procedures in the context of at-will employees, on the other hand, can be called voluntary procedures and were addressed as requests for reconsideration in chapter 2. You can tell that they are voluntary because they often have a disclaimer stating that the procedure does not change the fact that the employment relationship is at-will, but rather simply provides a mechanism to request a reconsideration. While not as powerful as a contractual or civil service grievance procedure, these at-will requests to reconsider still can be useful in exploring negotiation or revision of some decision if used diplomatically.

TIPS FOR USING A GRIEVANCE PROCEDURE

Grievance procedures often have steps. The first step may be filing a written grievance with your supervisor. Even if you feel that is pointless because the supervisor is the problem, you will need to do it in order to proceed. The second step may involve that supervisor's boss, and so on. Follow the steps, because if you skip one, you may forfeit your grievance. Also, when filing a grievance, keep the following tips in mind:

Timing

Every grievance procedure likely has a requirement that you file a grievance *within a set number of days* from the event about which you complain. I have helped employees with grievance procedures as speedy as five calendar days from the alleged wrong, while others have allowed fifteen to thirty or more days. You should know both the procedure and the deadline to file. If you miss the deadline, this often is called "untimely" and can mean you have waived any use of the grievance procedure.

Format

Some grievance procedures require a specific format, such as a letter to a supervisor or a union grievance form. One teachers' union contract, for example, requires the following format:

a. Name(s) and position(s) of the grievant(s)

b. A statement of the grievance and the facts involved, including relevant dates

c. A reference to the express provision(s) of this agreement allegedly misapplied, violated, or misinterpreted

d. The corrective action requested

e. Signature(s) of the grievant(s)

Form

In the above scenario, only a format is required. However, if a form is required, obtain it before you need it. Yet, whether form or format is required, if you don't follow the required procedure, your grievance can be dismissed on this ground alone, regardless of its substantive validity. In other words, an employer who opposes the substance of a grievance may take a close look at timing and other procedural defects to dismiss and therefore avoid addressing it.

FURTHER TIPS

First, have a copy of your grievance procedure and any forms required.

Second, if you turn in a grievance, keep a copy for your records.

Third, if you physically turn in your grievance, yet you cannot obtain a receipt, then send a copy by email with a short note saying that you turned it in and noting that, so as to be helpful, you are providing a convenient electronic copy. This "helpful" email will, of course, help you prove the grievance was submitted, if necessary.

GRIEVANCE PROCEDURES CAN BE POWERFUL PROCESSES WITH WHICH TO CHALLENGE ACTIONS TAKEN AGAINST YOU AT WORK.

Fourth, while your supervisor may have been wrong, don't let that tempt you to act rudely during any grievance process. Doing so is highly likely to offend, and your lack of self-control may suggest to the reviewer of the matter that your conduct was at fault.

CONCLUSION

Grievance procedures can be powerful processes with which to challenge actions taken against you at work. However, it is important to follow the steps, format, and timing they require so as to maximize their efficacy.

CHAPTER SIX

UNEMPLOYMENT BENEFITS

The State of Maryland established the unemployment benefit system to help employees who are laid off or terminated through no significant fault of their own. The state does this by providing unemployment benefits.

The benefits program should be construed for eligibility under law (see Hilder v. DLLR, 115 Md. App. 258, 280 (1996)). In other words, it should favor awarding employee benefits. However, the state can give employees a hard time and force proof of eligibility. Therefore, following the tips below will, quite literally, be to your benefit.

The provision of unemployment benefits has a host of requirements and is administered by the Maryland Department of Labor, Unemployment Benefits Division (referred to from here on as the Division). The Division issues monetary benefits to laid-off employees who meet the several requirements, including having worked for a sufficient length of time. Secondly, employees seeking unemployment benefits also must be ready and able to look for work, and third, they must do so. Unemployment benefits are for working people. You can't couch surf and continue to get them.

UNEMPLOYMENT BENEFITS ARE FOR WORKING PEOPLE. YOU CAN'T COUCH SURF AND CONTINUE TO GET THEM.

If, for example, an employer has laid you off for "business reasons," "poor performance," or because you're not a "good fit," the Division typically should provide unemployment benefits.

However, there are conditions and limitations to the receipt of such benefits where people are fired for legal misconduct or quit without good cause. For example, the state will dock weeks of benefits for what is deemed "misconduct" and might deny benefits entirely for "gross misconduct," both of which are defined below. Further, anyone who quits without "good cause" or "valid circumstance" will not be eligible for unemployment benefits.

Due to changing circumstances created by COVID-19, the impact of the pandemic on unemployment benefit law is not addressed here. Check with the Division for the latest on it.

TIMING TO FILE A CLAIM

If you work in Maryland, you can file for unemployment benefits after your work ends. In fact, the Division's website recommends that filing occur the day after the last day of work. If you wait, you still can file; however, eligibility for benefits includes the filing week and the week beforehand. So waiting risks the loss of benefits beyond that two-week retroactive period.

READYING YOUR CASE

While the Division often approves benefit applications that are not under dispute, it also scrutinizes cases in which it appears lawful to deny benefits, such as when the end of employment is due to misconduct, quitting, or other reason that causes denial of benefits.

By way of further example, someone who works two full-time jobs but loses one most likely earns too much to obtain unemployment benefits. You should, therefore, be prepared and heed the following suggestions when readying your case:

First, if you have performance awards, emails of praise or recognition, workplace awards and honors, a letter stating you have been "laid off for business reasons," and/or a strong résumé that shows a solid work history, have them handy. The Division handles thousands of cases; therefore, any evidence you can provide to support your claim will improve your chances of receiving benefits—if it is requested or necessary.

Second, if the Division asks for data or documents that it is lawfully allowed to request, provide them. In 2020, I worked on a case in which the Division asked an employee for wage history records. Typically, the Division has these on file; however, in this case it did not. When the employee was slow, it denied benefits. Also in 2020, I represented an employee who had quit for good cause and had a small pension that, to the Division, appeared to be taxable work-based income. This raised a red flag with the Division. However, after I provided the Division with a few pension pay stubs and other proof, the benefits were fast-tracked and approved. The takeaway: Don't assume the Division knows the specifics of your situation; provide documented information if requested.

Third, don't miss a Division phone call. The Division is supposed to call and/or send notice regarding your hearing in advance. If such a call or notice arrives a day before your call is scheduled, make room in your calendar. If you don't, the Division will typically deny benefits and force you to "appeal."

Fourth, if a medical or other emergency arises that necessitates you missing the call, obtain a notice providing an appeal right or new hearing. Then provide written reasons and/or proof of emergency (such as an emergency room hospital slip) to the Division by certified mail, which provides proof of delivery. Alternatively, if the Division accepts appeals by fax or email, you can file it so. Each of these automatically creates its own proof of transmission.

Fifth, keep a copy of everything you submit.

Sixth, make sure to file any appeal before the deadline via a means that provides proof of transmission.

MISCONDUCT

Misconduct is not specifically defined by the Division's controlling statute, but it generally means a violation of a known workplace policy, work rule, or duty. A finding of misconduct can disqualify a person for up to ten weeks of benefits (Md. Code, Lab. & Empl. § 8-1003).

Maryland's highest court has defined misconduct as "a transgression of some established rule or policy of the employer, the commission of a forbidden act, a dereliction of duty, or a course of wrongful conduct committed by an employee, within the scope of his employment relationship, during hours of employment, or on the employer's premises" (see Rogers v. Radio Shack, 271 Md. 126, 132, 314 A.2d 113, 117 (1974), quoting the Division). Sometimes the Division also calls this "simple misconduct," which should not be confused with poor performance. Further, the Division's online public digest, as of Jan. 6, 2021, clarifies that misconduct is not to be trivial and minor, writing: Misconduct "was not intended to include trivial or inconsequential acts or comments or isolated lapses in the employee's performance."

Misconduct, for example, does not occur in situations where an employer's policies are unclear on a matter salient to the issue at hand. If, for example, an employer fires an employee for behavior that the employer has no policy against or about which the employer's policy is unclear and then afterward contends that what the employee did was wrongful, a finding of misconduct will likely not be applicable. In Rogers v. Radio Shack, supra, for example, a retail store manager loaned a radio to a customer whose radio was in the shop for repair, just as some other store employees had done. The court rejected the employer's contention that this constituted misconduct because the employer had no clear policy prohibiting it.

Likewise, in Gilbert v. Mass Transit Administration, No. 654-BH-91, reported by the MD DOL Digest, the Maryland Transit Administration discharged an employee who missed work because she was arrested, contending that she should be denied unemployment benefits because she had called out for personal reasons and failed to disclose the arrest. The Division, however, found that the employer's rules were less than clear on this alleged duty of disclosure and so found no misconduct.

Even when an employer has a clear policy that the employee violates, the court will not necessarily find misconduct in every instance. In Day v. Sinai Hospital of Baltimore, No. 540-BH-85, reported by the MD DOL Digest, for example, an employee's bizarre reaction to a new medication created a disruption at work. As a result, the employee was discharged.

However, via medical documentation, the employee provided proven substantial explanation for the out-of-character incident, and so the Division did not find misconduct. However, everyday excuses often will not work. In Bush v. Becton Dickinson and Company, No. 2084-BR-94, reported by the MD DOL Digest, a mother's continually poor attendance at work due to child care qualified as simple misconduct because it repeatedly violated the employer's attendance policy and was deemed not an excuse.

GROSS MISCONDUCT

Gross misconduct is "deliberate and willful disregard" of an employer's interest. It includes "gross indifference" to an employer's interest or involves "repeated violations of employment rules" that demonstrate "wanton" intentional misconduct (Md. Code, Lab. & Empl. § 8-1002). Below are some examples.

In Employment Security Bd. v. LeCates, a supervisor came onto the employer's property without permission, took a work truck, drove it on a suspended license, caused an accident in Salisbury, Maryland, and returned the truck without reporting this chain of events. When his behavior was later discovered, it was found to constitute gross misconduct because the employee demonstrated both wanton indifference to and misuse of the employer's property (218 Md. 202, 145 A.2d 840 (1958)).

In Dept. of Economic & Empl. Dev. v. Jones, Maryland's highest court upheld a Division finding of gross misconduct where the violations of employer policy were less egregious than in LeCates, but nonetheless occurred repeatedly. In Jones, a dependable ten-year employee developed a substance abuse problem. He then failed many chances to correct his resulting behavior at work. The court upheld the Division's finding of gross misconduct because, after the problem came to the employer's attention and the employee was helped and additional changes were made, the employee failed five urinalysis drug tests, skipped other tests, and missed further work. This pattern of failures and problems demonstrated repeated (thus "gross") indifference to workplace rules and was therefore deemed to constitute gross misconduct. While the court decision indicates the Division had the authority to take the employee's drug addiction into greater consideration, the Division's discretion to not do so and find gross misconduct was upheld (79 Md. App. 531, 558 A.2d 739 (1989)).

CONTESTING MISCONDUCT

Burden of Proof

Employers have the burden to prove any level of misconduct and must present evidence to do so (see Ingram v. Laurel Fitness & Swim Club, Inc., No. 02290-BR-96, reported by the MD DOL Digest). Further, in Morgan v. The Webstaurant Store, Inc., a case that I handled, the Division's Board of Appeals emphasized that, in addition to misconduct, employers have the burden to prove gross misconduct (No. 01980-BR-17). In Morgan, the Board reversed a hearing decision denying benefits and granted benefits in full because the evidence was in "equipoise." In other words, the employer failed to prove gross misconduct, so a tie went to the employee and providing unemployment benefits.

Requesting Basic Fairness

Strict rules of evidence generally do not apply at administrative proceedings, such as those at the Division. However, the Division "must observe the basic rules of fairness as to parties appearing before them" (see Rogers v. Radio Shack, 271 Md. at 129, 314 A.2d at 115, quoting Dal Maso v. Board of Cnty. Comm'rs, 238, Md. 333, 337 (1965)).

As a result, the Division has leeway in construing the basic rules of fairness and so also can be reminded about what is basically fair. Let me provide one example. In a court of law, for instance, "hearsay" (which, speaking very generally, means testimony about what other people said) is inadmissible unless those other people come and say it, or a legal exception is met at court. Yet sometimes Division proceedings present hearsay. For example, a company HR representative might appear and recount what various supervisors and coworkers have said at work about a fired employee. In such situations, you can point out that hearsay is not in fact fair. The people should come and say it themselves. At least once, I have successfully argued that such hearsay should not be considered by the Division when granting or denying unemployment benefits.

FURTHER ISSUES

Good Cause to Quit

Generally, if you quit, you are not eligible for unemployment benefits unless you quit for "good cause." For instance, if you quit due to not being paid or due to sexual harassment, this will be considered "good cause" to quit and you should be awarded benefits (see Md. Code, Lab. & Empl., § 8-1001).

Additionally, quitting due to a documented medical condition can be a valid circumstance justifying an award of unemployment benefits if you had no other option but to take care of the medical condition and quit working (see Pearson v. Coca Cola Bottling Company, 2040-BH-83, MD DOL Digest—"An illness that has no connection with the work may still be a valid circumstance if the illness is a necessitous or compelling reason to leave work, and there is no reasonable alternative to quitting"). The federal court system also has recognized quitting due to severe discrimination to constitute good cause and what is called at court "constructive discharge" (see, e.g., Amirmokri v. Balt. Gas. & Elec. Co., 60 F.3d 1126 (4th Cir. 1995)).

Quitting for good cause always requires you to prove your case, whether it be with a doctor's note(s) or evidence of harassment (such as texts and emails, a complaint you've filed, evidence of not being paid [or not being paid overtime], and the like).

Forced Resignation

If your employer gives you the choice to either resign or be fired, this is considered the same as a termination in Maryland common law and so provides for unemployment benefits (see Cumberland & P. R. R. Co. v. Slack, 45 Md. 161, 172-175 (1876); Staggs v.

Blue Cross of Maryland, Inc., 61 Md. App. 381, 387, 486 A.2d 798, 801 (1985)).

However, you likely will need to explain this to the Division and should be prepared to do so by presenting any email or other document showing this was the choice presented to you. It is helpful to coordinate this with your employer if your employer is cooperative with you still.

WHEN DO YOU NEED A LAWYER?

Most people can file for unemployment benefits without a lawyer. Even if you are denied unemployment benefits and you believe the denial is a mistake, you may be able to file an appeal and handle the telephone interview (the next likely step) yourself. However, if the matter is tricky, obtaining a lawyer may be to your benefit. For example, if you seek benefits and the employer actively opposes it, you should likely at least consult with a lawyer. Doing so is less financially burdensome than you might expect, and any price charged can be weighed against the value of the twenty-six weeks of benefits at issue. Even if you cannot find representation, because these cases are not always cost effective for law firms to handle, you should consider a one-time legal consultation with an employment attorney to help you prepare.

CONCLUSION

From the outset of any dispute and throughout its resolution, being prepared with documentation, promptly responding to governmental communications, abiding by deadlines, and being honest are keys to success with the Division.

WORKERS' COMPENSATION

aryland's Workers' Compensation Law is an insurance program that most employers must pay into so that employees who are hurt at work can be compensated. Workers' compensation provides a partial payment of wages and coverage of medical expenses for work-related injuries, from the temporary to the permanent. It covers both accidental injuries at work and occupational diseases. Occupational disease, for instance, includes asbestos poisoning and black lung disease. Accidental injury includes any injury up to death arising from a workplace accident. Before our society implemented workers' compensation more than a century ago, if hurt at work, employees had to fend for themselves, negotiate a solution, or sue an employer in an uphill battle against a usually better-funded adversary. Now, however, there is a complicated bureaucracy set up to process these claims under the Workers' Compensation Commission of the State of Maryland.

NOTIFICATION DEADLINES

Notification of Accident

If hurt at work in an accident, you need to act promptly. According to the law, if personally injured at work, you have only ten days to notify your employer, either verbally or in writing (Md. Code, Lab. & Empl. §9-704 (2021)). As previously stated, in such a situation, a written notice that you keep a copy of provides the most protection (should you ever need it) because it can prove notice. Further after notifying your employer, you must file any claim for workers' compensation within sixty days of the accident (Md. Code, Lab. & Empl. §9-704).

There can be mitigating considerations that may factor into these rigid time requirements. If, for example, you can show good cause for a delay beyond sixty days, you may be permitted up to two years to file the claim. However, an employer can argue that such a delay significantly prejudices them, and if so, obtain a procedural denial. An employer, for instance, might argue that such "improper delay" shows why a claim should not be paid, either in full or in part (*Id.* at §9-706). Further, after two years from the injury date, any unfiled claim is "completely barred" (*Id.* at §9-709).

Notification of Occupational Disease/ Injuries Resulting in Death

Occupational diseases as well as injuries resulting in death each have different time frames within which you must notify your employer. Occupational diseases are considered to be problems that develop over the long term. You therefore have a year after finding out you have one (or after you should have found out about it) to provide notification (*Id.* at §9-705). As for injuries resulting in death, there are different time frames within which families of employees who die at work from injury may bring workers' compensation claims (*Id.* at §9-710). Note that dealing with a workplace death of a loved one is a serious matter. Therefore, if you are a family member in this situation, seeking legal advice is highly advisable so as to ensure meeting deadlines and best pursuing legal redress.

PROTECTING YOUR RIGHTS

Hiring an Attorney

Maryland's workers' compensation law is highly regulatory, and the forms the Commission requires you to file are highly specific. Therefore, they may be difficult for you to understand. If everything goes smoothly, the matter is simple, and the employer is helpful, you may be able to handle it all yourself or with the help of your employer's human resources department. However, if your employer challenges it in any way, or if it is complicated or you need help understanding your legal rights and available remedies, you can find a workers' compensation attorney to help and/or represent you.

In Baltimore County v. Quinlan, 466 Md. 1, 19 (2019), for example, Maryland's Court of Appeals expanded the scope of claims to more easily recognize occupational diseases that occur over decades. In Quinlan, medical experts traced an EMT's degenerative knee condition and correlated it to his job. This is the kind of complex matter that requires skilled representation by an employment or workers' compensation attorney, medical experts, and legal team.

A Sad but True Story

One sad workers' compensation case involved a former truck mechanic. The mechanic had hurt his back while under a truck at work performing a repair. Realizing he had a serious injury, he'd informed HR via text message. This text message constitutes the notice of the injury discussed earlier in the chapter. Then he'd quit because he felt he was too hurt to work. The mechanic was unaware that he was eligible to file for workers' compensation, and no one told him. Therefore, the mechanic simply walked away with what turned out to be the last straw for his bad back and no compensation whatsoever.

HE SOUGHT THESE BENEFITS, BUT BEING SO LATE, IT WAS VERY DIFFICULT TO PROVE HIS CASE. HE RECEIVED VERY LITTLE COMPENSATION. KNOW AND PROTECT YOUR RIGHTS.

Almost two years later and just before the two-year legal statutory deadline passed, this mechanic finally obtained legal help. He sought these benefits, but being so late, it was very difficult to prove his case. He received very little compensation. Know and protect your rights.

MARYLAND LAW PROTECTS THE RIGHT TO SEEK WORKERS' COMPENSATION

Finally, Maryland makes it illegal to fire someone for filing a workers' compensation claim (Md. Code, Lab. & Empl. § 9-1105 (2021)). As the law says, "a person who violates this section is guilty of a misdemeanor and on conviction is subject to a fine not exceeding $500 or imprisonment not exceeding 1 year or both" (*Id.* at § 9-1105(b)). However, these wrongful termination cases have, to date, proven difficult to win at court. For more on this, see also chapter 13, where the legal claim of wrongful termination is further covered.

CONCLUSION

If you are injured at work, you have a right to seek workers' compensation to provide you with medical expenses and a percentage of lost wages as applicable. This covers occupational diseases as well as "accidental personal injury" at work (Md. Code, Lab. & Empl. §9-501(a) (2021); accord Harris v. Bd. of Educ., 375 Md. 21 (2003)). As stated by the Maryland Court of Appeals, "employees who follow the procedural rules of the Act and can prove they were injured while working can almost certainly recover compensation to prevent undue hardships caused by loss of wages and medical expenses" (Harris v. Bd. of Educ., 375 Md. 21, 58-59 (2003)).

CHAPTER EIGHT

LEAVE POLICIES AND DISABILITY LEAVE

MHWFA, FMLA, and ADA

There is an intersection of laws that relate to leave and disability in Maryland. This chapter touches upon a few of them.

MARYLAND LEAVE LAWS

Sick Leave

In 2018, Maryland passed the Maryland Healthy Working Families Act (MHWFA). The act requires employers with fifteen or more employees to provide *paid* "sick and safe" leave that accrues as you work. For employers of fourteen employees or less, however, sick leave can be unpaid. Of course, if the employer simply provides the required amount before it accrues, thereby not requiring such accrual, this, too, would satisfy the law in advance. Certain select industries are exempted. Plus, some local jurisdictions have specific sick leave laws that are additional to the state's—for example, the counties of Montgomery and Prince George's. These local laws are not covered here.

Your Employer's Leave Policies

As noted in chapter 2, your employee handbook may provide an employer-based leave policy that might not be legally enforceable at court but still provides leave options under employer-specific programs, including maternity leave, educational pursuits, extended personal leave, and for sundry purposes.

Of course, if leave policies are granted to some employees yet denied to others for an illegal discriminatory reason, this may violate local, state and/or federal discrimination law.

Family Medical Leave

The US Family and Medical Leave Act (FMLA) applies to employers of fifty or more employees and only applies to employees after they have worked twelve months or more. Further, these employees must have worked 1,250 work hours or more during that time (which equals almost full-time).

If an employee satisfies FMLA prerequisites, the FMLA ensures an employee up to twelve weeks of unpaid leave for a "serious medical condition" and requires an employer to maintain the employee's health insurance during FMLA leave (see FMLA, 29 U.S.C. § 2601 et seq. (2021)).

Family medical leave also protects an employee's right to take time off to care for an immediate family member, including a parent, spouse, or child. It does not, however, require a grant of protected time off to care for a non-immediate family member (for instance, an aunt, unless she raised you as a de facto parent). In addition, the FMLA covers leave triggered by the birth of a child to care for that child. It covers intermittent leave, which is extra unpaid time off to care for a chronic condition. For example, time needed for bed rest, doctor visits, and treatments related to ongoing serious medical conditions is a permissible use of FMLA leave (see F.M.L.A., 29 U.S.C. § 2612).

I have helped people with intermittent FMLA leave on file to obtain time off for chronic migraines, periodic lupus, and chronic asthma flare-ups, for instance.

IF YOU HAVE REQUESTED FMLA LEAVE AND ARE HAVING PROBLEMS ACQUIRING IT, THE FIRST STEP IS TO MAKE SURE THAT YOUR REQUEST IS ISSUED IN WRITING.

FMLA can be complex. Consequently, if you have requested FMLA leave and are having problems acquiring it, the first step is to make sure that your request is issued in writing, whether by email, letter, or otherwise. Further, where possible, the FMLA requires thirty days (or more) advance notice (see F.M.L.A., 29 U.S.C. § 2612(e)). The employer is required to respond in writing if denying the FMLA leave request. Emergency FMLA use also is permissible if justified by an actual unforeseeable medical event.

The FMLA also protects the employee's right to return to their job or to equivalent job unless the employee is a top-earning, essential employee designated as "key," as is discussed further below (see 29 U.S.C. § 2614). Employers may replace certain higher paid, key employees to protect themselves from grievous harm (see 29 U.S.C. § 2614(b); 29 C.F.R. § 825.217). If you are one of these key employees, you must receive advance written notice of this refusal of restoration due to grievous harm requiring the employer to fill the position.

An employer who tries to prevent an employee from returning to work by alleging malfeasance often is accused of interfering with the exercise of an FMLA legal right to return and/or retaliating (see 29 U.S.C. § 2615). This being said, if the employer has documented the alleged malfeasance (which, for example, might include negligence on the job or workplace theft) and if the allegation is true, then that employer can legally fire that person regardless of the FMLA. Usually, such terminations are executed after the leave expires. This makes them tricky because the timing appears suspicious.

Any FMLA lawsuit should be filed within two years of the alleged violation. The law requires proof of "willful violation" if filing after two years and within three years of the alleged violation. After three years, the right to sue is waived without exceptional equitable excuse, such as having been in a coma in a hospital and unable to hire counsel and file a lawsuit. An aggrieved employee also can file a complaint with the US Department of Labor (29 U.S.C. § 2617).

FMLA AND NOTICE

Making the Request

In my experience, many disputes under the FMLA involve lack of notice. The act requires employers to provide employees with notice of their FMLA status and eligibility—that is, their federal FMLA rights—when leave is requested or the status queried (see US D.O.L. Reg., 29 CFR § 825.300(b)). Yet I have handled several disputes in which employees who requested FMLA notification from HR were either not provided with it or had their requests denied, with the result that their leave was either prevented or delayed. Additionally, I was involved with an FMLA dispute at a local municipal government in which HR continually denied an employee's FMLA papers. This was likely for some unknown reason. HR thus used minor errors to keep sending them back without technically denying the leave on the merits. I was able to resolve it through careful documentation, especially of all communications and transmissions among us.

Upon receipt of an FMLA request, an employer must provide, within five business days, written notice of eligibility to take FMLA leave or denial of eligibility (see *id.* at (b)(1)-(2)). This being said, if you make a request orally and you do not follow up with, at the very least, a confirmatory email, then it is easy to deny ever hearing, receiving, or remembering the request. Even in a cooperative workplace, one in which employees and employers communicate verbally and on friendly terms, one can send a confirmatory email without appearing to be a stickler or raise any red flags. All one needs to say is something to the effect of "Beth, thank you for taking my FMLA request on Monday. I look forward to receiving the forms soon."

What Is Proper Notice?

Again, if requested to do so, an employer also has a legal duty to provide an employee with any required FMLA forms (see *id.* at (c)). Further, in response to queries, the employer also is required by law to issue a notice of ineligibility and/or limited eligibility (see *id.* at (b)-(c)).

However, in cases where an employee has used other forms of leave, such as sick pay, employer leave, and/or vacation pay, but has not done so under the auspices of the FMLA, an employer cannot deny eligibility by retroactively designating such leave as "FMLA leave." The US Department of Labor has declared such surprise "retroactive designation" illegal (see US D.O.L. Reg., 29 CFR § 825.301(d)).

Employers also cannot retract notice of FMLA availability based on mere mistake as to eligibility if the employee has already relied upon it to take leave. Federal courts have held that such surprise is inequitable and constitutes unlawful interference with the FMLA (see Miller v. Pers.-Touch of Va., Inc., 342 F. Supp. 2d 499, 513-15 (E.D. Va. 2004); Szostek v. Drexel Univ., No. 12-2921, 2013 US Dist. LEXIS 177275, at *21-25 (E.D. Pa. Dec. 16, 2013)).

DISABILITY LEAVE: ADA AND FMLA

The FMLA covers a "serious medical condition" and sometimes this also concerns a "disability" as defined by the US Americans with Disabilities Act (ADA) and further discussed in chapter 9. If so, the FMLA and the ADA overlap.

FOR A NEW EMPLOYEE, THE ADA CAN PROVIDE LEGAL RIGHTS IMMEDIATELY, WHILE THE FMLA KICKS IN ONLY AFTER TWELVE MONTHS.

For a new employee, the ADA can provide legal rights immediately, while the FMLA kicks in only after twelve months. However, the ADA, as federal law, is limited to covering employers with fifteen or more employees. The ADA requires employers to consider any "reasonable accommodation" for a qualified disabled employee.

This can include forms of unpaid leave from work even after FMLA leave expires. But what is reasonable additional leave? It depends. By law, it should not cause the employer an undue hardship. The issues of a reasonable accommodation and what is a disability under the ADA are addressed in chapter 9.

This being said, Maryland's federal courts have determined that "finite" leave—that is, leave for some set amount of time—is a requirement of a reasonable ADA leave request. Therefore, an indefinite and vague request for leave, if not clarified through a dialogue (designated under the ADA as the "interactive process"), can be denied and an employee justifiably laid off (see Wilson v. Dollar Gen. Corp., 717 F.3d 337 (4th Cir. 2013)).

For example, in Rodgers v. Lehman 869 F.2d 253 (D. Md. 1989), a Maryland federal court held that two to four weeks of leave for navy personnel undergoing alcohol rehabilitation treatment was reasonable. It also indicated this timeframe was very likely reasonable in many circumstances. Yet, in Moore v. Maryland Dept. of Pub. Safety & Corr. Services Patuxent Inst., Civ. No. CCB-11-0553, 2013 WL 549864 (D. Md. Feb. 13, 2013), a correctional officer at a large statewide governmental employer received a year of leave. However, she was lawfully let go when she both failed to adequately communicate her return date and requested more leave in an open-ended manner. Again, the issue of a reasonable accommodation is further addressed in the next chapter.

CONCLUSION

Matters of employment leave, disability, and medical leave involve an intersection of federal, state, and local laws, as well as any leave policies specific to the employer. The next chapter takes a closer look at leave and other requests for relief as a reasonable accommodation under the ADA.

CHAPTER NINE

REASONABLE ACCOMMODATIONS FOR QUALIFIED DISABLED EMPLOYEES

The US Americans with Disabilities Act (ADA), 42 US Code § 12101 et seq., "is designed to level the playing field for the more than 43,000,000 Americans who have one or more physical or mental disabilities" (Schmidt v. Methodist Hosp. of Indiana, Inc., 89 F.3d 342, 344 (7th Cir. 1996)).

HOW DOES THE ADA DEFINE DISABILITY?

As defined under the ADA, a disability is a complex matter. This being said, put simply, an ADA disability is "a physical or mental impairment that substantially limits one or more major life activities of such individual" (42 US Code § 12102). Further, generally, such disabilities are usually chronic, permanent, or last for some time. However, no strict minimal duration of disability is now required under the law.

The definition of a disability under the ADA also includes the following additional categories compared to an actual disability: (1) The ADA protects employees who have a "record" of disability, whether or not the disability itself meets the requirements of the ADA, as well as (2) those whom employers perceive as being disabled even if not actually disabled (*Id.*).

To illustrate, someone may have an anxiety disorder that causes them problems, or maybe they see a therapist, but it does not substantially limit one or more major life activities and so is not an actual disability under the ADA. However, if the employer finds out and treats them as disabled, this still can constitute illegal disability discrimination based on perceived disability. For the purposes of this guide, however, I address only actual disability below.

WHO DOES THE ADA PROTECT?

The ADA applies to employers with fifteen or more employees and protects "qualified disabled" people. This means it does not protect all disabled people who meet the ADA definition of "disability" but cannot work. Rather, it protects disabled people who can work and perform the job with and/or without a reasonable accommo-

IT PROTECTS DISABLED PEOPLE WHO CAN WORK AND PERFORM THE JOB WITH AND/OR WITHOUT A REASONABLE ACCOMMODATION.

dation. Some disabled people need a reasonable accommodation to perform their jobs, and they are protected. Others do not need it and remain protected from disability discrimination under the ADA.

The ADA also requires that a charge be filed to protect and enforce one's ADA legal rights, a time-sensitive process with deadlines that is covered in chapter 10.

Maryland's similar disability protections are located at Title 20, Section 606 of the Government Article of the Maryland Code. For brevity, this guide will focus on the federal law as applied in Maryland.

WHAT IS A "REASONABLE ACCOMMODATION" AND WHAT DOES IT INVOLVE?

As discussed briefly in chapter 8, leave can be considered an ADA reasonable accommodation; however, the definition of "reasonable accommodation" depends on the particular workplace and the specific job at hand. Concerning leave from work, courts have determined that leave without any foreseeable end date is unreasonable and can be denied.

However, whether requesting leave or some other accommodation, the law does not require employees to have a solution wrapped as a present and tied with a bow when speaking to their employer. Rather, an employee should make a request. Then, the law requires both sides to engage in a flexible interactive process to try to make it work.

THE INTERACTIVE PROCESS

Federal law requires employees who request reasonable accommodation to engage in a dialogue that the ADA terms an "interactive process." Under Maryland law, however, such dialogue is called an "individualized assessment." Both terms mean that the employer has to at least discuss the requested accommodation with you and determine whether it is possible. Maryland courts have interpreted the individualized assessment as being slightly different from the federal interactive process and slightly more individualized and robust.

The process of dialogue about a reasonable accommodation makes sense under the structure of both the ADA and Maryland's disability rights equivalent because what is reasonable or an undue burden is fact-specific to each workplace. Thus, even if a requested accommodation is not ultimately provided, it needs to at least be discussed to satisfy an employer's legal duty. Under the ADA, accommodation need only be reasonable, must not pose undue hardship to the employer, and dialogue about it must be conducted in good faith (see Jacobs v. N.C. Admin. Office of the Courts, 780 F.3d 562, 581 (4th Cir. 2015)—interpreting 29 C.F.R. § 1630.2(o)(3)); see also Peninsula Reg'l Med. Ctr. v. Adkins, 448 Md. 197, 137 A.3d 211 (2016)—on Maryland's individual assessment process).

Examples of Reasonable and Unreasonable Accommodations

Following are some examples of reasonable and unreasonable accommodation.

Teleworking is becoming a more acceptable accommodation. However, it may be more reasonable for someone working in an office to request an accommodation to work remotely than it would be for someone working as a store clerk. Further, if someone is having performance problems, this can become a valid reason to deny telework because the employer may believe that more on-site supervision is needed. Additionally, a chicken-and-the-egg situation can develop if an employee needs an accommodation but postpones requesting it until after developing performance problems.

The ADA provides a right to seek reassignment to a vacant position for a qualified disabled employee. For example, an EMT officer who, after many years on the job, had sustained torn rotator cuffs, sought to move to a vacant office support position. The officer had a right to express consideration for the vacancy. However, the employer denied his request and instructed him to apply via the company's internal application pool (in other words, to get in line). The court deemed the instruction an illegal denial of the ADA reasonable accommodation process that should have fast-tracked this employee over outside applicants (Shapiro v. Twp. of Lakewood, 292 F.3d 356 (3d Cir. 2002)).

A textile worker with badly arthritic knees who worked in a factory with concrete floors had an ADA right to request assignment to the company's wood-floor production plant so long as there were vacancies (EEOC v. Stowe-Pharr Mills, Inc., 216 F.3d 373, 379 (4th Cir. 2000)).

A one-armed police officer in Baltimore County was informally accommodated for several years with an office position. However, when the department was reorganized, office positions were limited to a set term for any injured officer, and the officer's time then expired once he served that same set term after the reorganization occurred. Further, the department successfully argued to the court that a patrol position could not accommodate a one-armed officer. As a result, the county's decision to let that disabled officer go was upheld as legal under the ADA, in part because the officer was granted equal rights and the ADA does not require creating a permanent office job just for him (see Champ v. Balt. Cty., 884 F. Supp. 991 (D. Md. 1995); affirmed Champ v. Balt. Cnty, No. 95-2061, Slip Op., 1996 WL 383924 (4th Cir. 1996)).

In Tyndall v. Nat'l Educ. Ctrs., 31 F.3d 209 (4th Cir. 1994), the Fourth Circuit upheld an employer's denial of a teacher's request for accommodation of more leave due to lupus primarily because her prior history of chronic tardiness and absences evidenced it would prove futile, and no solution would enable her to teach. Her employer also argued that the educational setting required in-person teaching. Of course, in 2021, the prevalence of online teaching might change what is reasonably available to this teacher.

In Reyazuddin v. Montgomery Cty., 789 F.3d 407 (4th Cir. 2015), the Fourth Circuit held that a blind call center employee's request that her employer, Montgomery County, provide special software enabling her, as an ADA-qualified disabled person, to work at the call center could be reasonable, depending on the cost. Therefore, the case was sent back to the trial court for further adjudication of the cost and its reasonableness or not.

FURTHER DISCUSSION

Employees' success in seeking reasonable accommodation varies and may depend not only on what is deemed reasonable but also on their own ability to communicate. In my experience, the ability to communicate, an employer's financial well-being, the personality and concerns of immediate supervisors, and the skills of HR all affect how these requests are handled. The above cases illustrate how legal, interpersonal, and logistical concerns come into play to affect what is an interactive and applied legal right under the ADA. As a result, these cases provide guidance only for anyone to think about their own needs and their workplace.

CONCLUSION

The ADA is a vast topic. This guide just touches on it. In general, under the ADA, reasonable accommodations are legally required for qualified disabled employees unless they cause an undue hardship. Employees also should remember that disability rights law requires employees themselves to take a reasonable approach to requesting accommodation as well as requiring the same of employers. This means considering both your own and your employer's needs. So if you are a working disabled person, you should study your legal rights and obtain legal advice when and if necessary.

CHAPTER TEN

DISCRIMINATION, RETALIATION, AND FILING CHARGES

DISCRIMINATION

Discrimination on the basis of race, national origin, religion, color, and/or sex—five major protected classes—is illegal under Title VII of the Civil Rights Act of 1964, as amended (see 42 U.S.C. § 2000(e) et seq. (2021)). The concept of "sex" discrimination includes gender discrimination, which, under federal law, has been extended to protect sexual orientation and gender identity (see Bostock v. Clayton County, 140 S. Ct. 1731 (decided June 15, 2020)).

Maryland also protects all of these categories under a single state statutory law and includes additionally marital status, age, genetic information, and disability as a basis upon which one cannot be discriminated against at work (see Md. Code, Ann., St. Gov. § 20-606 (2021)).

Further, both federal and Maryland law protect people against age and disability discrimination. The US Age Discrimination in Employment Act of 1967 (ADEA), 29 U.S.C. § 621 et seq., defines the protected category of "age" as someone forty and older and covers employers with twenty or more employees. Maryland law, on the other hand, does not define age by status and so arguably protects even young people from discrimination due to age. It also covers employers with fifteen employees or more (see Md. Code, Ann., St. Gov. §§ 20-606 & 20-601(d) (2021)). Additionally, pregnancy discrimination is illegal under both state and federal law, handled often as a form of gender discrimination. These are the primary common categories of discrimination, and further federal and state laws on discrimination shall not be covered in this chapter.

How the law works also depends on how courts handle and interpret these legal terms. Such interpretations are not simple. They also change over time. For instance, in Oncale v. Sundowner Offshore Services,

523 US 75 (1998), a case that lower federal courts had dismissed, the US Supreme Court reversed the lower courts and held that a male oil rig worker accused of not being "man enough" and then harassed faced illegal gender stereotype discrimination. Gender stereotype discrimination is a form of gender discrimination (for example, when a woman is punished for being too bossy and/or not feminine enough) if it hurts an employee's chances of promotion, for instance, or results in some other significant adverse employment action. A denial of female executive's career advancement due to being "too aggressive" as a form of discrimination was successfully presented in Price Waterhouse v. Hopkins, 490 US 228 (1989). The same aggressive behavior held against her was expected from male counterparts at work.

For more information about protected categories in general, as well as more information about the scope of those listed above, you will need to consult the law. Also, note that when seeking action on the basis of discrimination, it is wise to obtain professional legal advice.

RETALIATION

Retaliation is the legal term for when an employer takes a dissuasive employment action against an employee who opposes being discriminated against at work, participates in a process to redress illegal discrimination, or otherwise stands up for their related antidiscrimination rights. This dissuasive employment action to constitute retaliation must be significant, such as when an employer demotes, reduces someone's pay, fires, suspends someone without pay, or denies a not-trivial benefit of work due to "protected activity" (see Burlington Northern & Santa Fe (BNSF) Railway Co. v. White, 548 U.S. 53 (2006)).

DISCIPLINE IN DISCRIMINATION AND RETALIATION CLAIMS

As discussed in chapter 2, when standing alone, the progressive discipline policy in an employee handbook often is not legally enforceable. However, how an employer uses it may constitute evidence of discrimination. For instance, some employers may discipline employees in a protected class "by the book" while being more lenient with comparable others outside of it.

What makes employees comparable under the law? This requires an analysis specific to each workplace. Generally speaking, employees who share the same job title, worksite, time at work as coworkers, same supervisor(s), and have primarily similar allegations of workplace violations very likely can be legally compared to determine if an illegal discriminatory reason accounts for the disparities at issue (see Cook v. CSX Transp. Corp., 988 F.2d 507 (4th Cir. 1993); Haynes v. Waste Connections, Inc., 922 F.3d 219, 223-224 (4th Cir. 2019)).

Example of Illegal Discrimination in At-Will Employment

In the at-will employment relationship, what is unfair is not necessarily illegal discrimination. Employees can, for instance, be fired for wearing blue socks, for not wearing socks, or simply because the owner has a bad day, if working at-will. As discussed in chapter 1, an at-will employee can be fired for a good reason, a bad reason, or for no reason at all, but not for an illegal reason. Unfair as it may seem, for instance, firing an at-will employee so as to replace them with a family member is almost certainly legal, if nepotism is the motive.

THE PROGRESSIVE DISCIPLINE POLICY IN AN EMPLOYEE HANDBOOK OFTEN IS NOT LEGALLY ENFORCEABLE. HOWEVER, HOW AN EMPLOYER USES IT MAY CONSTITUTE EVIDENCE OF DISCRIMINATION.

In this broadly permissive context of at-will employment, proving illegal discrimination often requires persistence, painstaking detail, and very specific analysis. For instance, in Farryn Johnson v. Harborplace Hooters (MCCR 2013), an African American waitress at a Hooters restaurant in Baltimore City was allegedly fired for having green hair, while Caucasian waitresses with neon-colored, cool hair were permitted to work. Was this racist, insofar as what was "cool" for Caucasian waitresses was not "cool" for an African American? The case, which progressed to arbitration, where it was decided in 2015, deemed it illegal, calling the firing "racial discrimination." Because the case was not handled by a court of law, specific rationales for the decision were not published. However, it might be speculated that at least part of the rationale was racial stereotyping, as the facts fit that description.

EMPLOYER SIZE IS IMPORTANT

The size of your employer has important ramifications on your right to file a claim of discrimination. Title VII of the Civil Rights Act of 1964 only applies to employers with fifteen employees or more in at least twenty weeks of the current or preceding calendar year for when the wrong occurred (see 42 U.S.C.

§ 2000(e)(b)). The federal age discrimination law applies to employers with twenty or more employees during at least twenty calendar weeks (see 29 US Code § 630(b)). And Maryland discrimination law applies to employers at the fifteen-employee threshold (see Md. Code, Gov. Art. § 20-601(d)(A)—although "harassment" claims that are based on illegal discrimination now apply to any employer with one or more employee. *Id.* (d)(B)).

Therefore, if you work for a smaller employer and believe you are being discriminated against, these laws may not apply. However, there may be local county ordinances and city codes with similar protections that do, including in Howard County, Baltimore County, Prince George's and Montgomery Counties, and in Baltimore City, Maryland, among other jurisdictions. Smaller employers, for example, also may be subject to Maryland common and/or constitutional laws, as well as to other federal laws. So if you work at a smaller employer and none of the federal or state laws applies, you will need to refer to local, common, and/or constitutional law to know whether you have a case.

FILING CHARGES OF DISCRIMINATION

If you believe you have been unlawfully discriminated or retaliated against, and if either Title VII, Maryland law, or a local law applies, then you must file a charge of discrimination with a US, Maryland, or local civil rights agency, which will investigate and seek a remedy. The same charge can cover both discrimination and retaliation.

If you do not file a charge of discrimination or retaliation within three hundred days under US federal law, or within 180 days under Maryland law, you give up the related legal rights under Title VII of the US Civil Rights Act of 1964 and under Maryland's equivalent law at Md. Code, Ann., St. Gov. § 20-606 (the local laws are not further covered here).

To file a charge in the State of Maryland, you can choose to file it with the Maryland Commission on Civil Rights and/or the US Equal Employment Opportunity Commission, or with a local jurisdiction agency. The statewide agencies are located in Baltimore at:

US EQUAL EMPLOYMENT
OPPORTUNITY COMMISSION
GH FALLON FEDERAL BUILDING
31 HOPKINS PLAZA, SUITE 1432
BALTIMORE, MD 21201
UNITED STATES
https://www.eeoc.gov/field-office/baltimore/location

MARYLAND COMMISSION ON CIVIL
RIGHTS
WILLIAM DONALD SCHAEFER TOWER
6 SAINT PAUL STREET, SUITE 900
BALTIMORE, MD 21202-1631
https://mccr.maryland.gov/Pages/Contact-Us.aspx

The statewide agencies practice what they call cross-filing. If you file at one of them listed above, it is automatically cross-filed at the other to proceed under both state and federal law as applicable.

CHARGE OF DISCRIMINATION

This form is affected by the Privacy Act of 1974; See Privacy Act Statement before completing

AGENCY	CHARGE NUMBER
☐ FEPA ☐ EEOC	

MARYLAND COMMISSION ON HUMAN RELATIONS	and EEOC

State or local Agency, if any

NAME (Indicate Mr., Ms., Mrs.)	HOME TELEPHONE (Include Area Code)

STREET ADDRESS	CITY, STATE AND ZIP CODE	DATE OF BIRTH

NAMED IS THE EMPLOYER, LABOR ORGANIZATION, EMPLOYMENT AGENCY, APPRENTICESHIP COMMITTEE, STATE OR LOCAL GOVERNMENT AGENCY WHO DISCRIMINATED AGAINST ME (If more than one list below.)

NAME	NUMBER OF EMPLOYEES, MEMBERS	TELEPHONE (Include Area Code)

STREET ADDRESS	CITY, STATE AND ZIP CODE	COUNTY

SAMPLE ONLY / ILLUSTRATIVE PURPOSE

CAUSE OF DISCRIMINATION BASED ON (Check appropriate box(es))

☐ RACE ☐ COLOR ☐ SEX ☐ RELIGION ☐ AGE

☐ RETALIATION ☐ NATIONAL ORIGIN ☐ DISABILITY ☐ OTHER (Specify)

DATE DISCRIMINATION TOOK PLACE EARLIEST (ADEA/EPA)

☐ CONTINUING ACTION

THE PARTICULARS ARE (If additional paper is needed, attach extra sheet(s)):

1.
2.
3.
4.
5.
6.
7.
8.
9.
10.

I want this charge filed with both the EEOC and the State or local Agency, if any. I will advise the agencies if I change my address or telephone number and I will cooperate fully with them in the processing of my charge in accordance with their procedures.

X

I declare under penalty of perjury that the foregoing is true and correct.

X

Date   Charging Party (Signature)

NOTARY - (When necessary for State and Local Requirements)

I swear or affirm that I have read the above charge and that it is true to the best of my knowledge, information and belief.

SIGNATURE OF COMPLAINANT

X

SUBSCRIBED AND SWORN TO BEFORE ME THIS DATE (Day, month, and year)

EEOC FORM 5 (Rev. 12/93)

I want this charge filed with both the EEOC and the State or local Agency, if any. I will advise the agencies if I change my address or telephone number and I will cooperate fully with them in the processing of my charge in accordance with their procedures.

X

I declare under penalty of perjury that the foregoing is true and correct.

X

Date   Charging Party (Signature)

Signature section:
Both boxes must be signed for the Charge to be filed.

HARASSMENT CLAIMS IN MARYLAND

Harassment is a form of discrimination or retaliation and therefore also requires that a charge be filed. Generally speaking, harassment must be "severe" and "pervasive" to constitute an "adverse employment action" and be actionable. It involves an intolerable workplace. The courts as well as agency investigators will not consider mere workplace inconvenience or being given the "cold shoulder" to constitute harassment because it is both amorphous and less than intolerable.

Maryland recently expanded its jurisdiction over harassment. The law now applies to discriminatory harassment (and possibly also retaliatory harassment) by any employer in the state with one or more employees. It also holds employers accountable by including conduct by an employer's "agent" too (see Md. Code, Ann., St. Gov. § 20-601(d) (2021)).

Court precedent on harassment is extensive and requires highly specific legal consideration that escapes the scope of this guide. Nevertheless, here are some examples:

In Amirmokri v. Balt. Gas. & Elec. Co., 60 F.3d 1126 (4th Cir. 1995), an engineer complained of national origin discrimination. The engineer contended that over several months his coworkers had called him inflammatory, derogatory names related to his Middle Eastern national origin. When hired, he also had been promised a fast-track to promotion that never materialized. The case details the engineer's complaints to management about the harassment, management's refusal to address the problem, and the engineer's ensuing documented anxiety and stress-related illness, which forced him to quit on his doctor's advice. This harassment occurred for about a year, caused documented medical mental health injury, and therefore met the legal threshold for severe and pervasive harassment due to his national origin.

In contrast, in Gunten v. Maryland, 243 F.3d 858, 869 (4th Cir. 2001), an employee filed a hostile work environment retaliation claim alleging that, after having pursued a discrimination charge, her coworkers gave her the cold shoulder, and she was supervised more closely and relocated to a basement desk. The court, however, found these alleged conditions were neither severe nor pervasive enough to constitute illegal harassment. Further, it found that the basement desk, while perhaps not her preference, still permitted her to work effectively.

The Gunten decision is a good example of how

retaliation may play out in the workplace, and I see these situations in my practice of law. In such a situation, I likely advise a go-slow approach. Work on documentation first before proceeding with any claim. Consider what might be done within the confines of employment to address it, including requesting a change of workplace location and/or supervisors, or some other remedy, as well as looking for another job.

This all is because the type of hostility at work illustrated in Gunten is "in the atmosphere," so to speak. Therefore, it is difficult to prove and simply may be not

WORK ON DOCUMENTATION FIRST BEFORE PROCEEDING WITH ANY CLAIM.

"severe" and "pervasive" enough to constitute illegal harassment under the law.

SECTION 1981 AND 1983 CLAIMS

A provision of the federal Civil Rights Act of 1866 makes racial discrimination illegal in the US and applies to any private-sector employer (see 42 U.S.C. §1981). Likewise, a provision of the federal Civil Rights Act of 1871 makes it illegal to discriminate based on race and can be applied to state and local governments if a government adopts policies and widespread practices that are discriminatory (see 42 U.S.C. §1983).

Such provisions, which arise from post-Civil War attempts to redress racism after the abolishment of US slavery, have evolved to cover various applications, including protecting various races from discrimination. It is beyond the scope of this guide to discuss this. However, discrimination actions that rely on these acts do not require filing the discussed administrative charges. For more information, you can research these laws online, through periodicals and textbooks, as well as by consulting a lawyer.

CAPS ON DAMAGES IN TITLE VII DISCRIMINATION AND RETALIATION CLAIMS

Title VII of the Civil Rights Act of 1964 and Maryland's state law counterpart both cap compensatory and punitive damages available to wronged employees, which are forms of damages beyond actual lost wages and legal expenses. These caps apply based upon a private-sector employer's size. In cases in which actual economic losses are small, this may greatly impact a legal claim. In contrast, these caps have less overall impact on cases in which discrimination or retaliation has resulted in significant loss of wages, loss of a pension, or loss of other economic benefits.

The caps for combined compensatory and punitive damages, concerning private-sector employers, are as follows:

- 15 to 100 employees—$50,000

- 101 to 200 employees—$100,000

- 201 to 500 employees—$200,000

- 501 or more employees—$300,000

See 42 U.S.C. §1981a(b)(3) (2021); Md. Code, St. Gov. §§ 20-1009, 20-1013 (2021).

When seeking damages from a local, state, or federal government, further complex laws apply, including governmental immunities beyond the scope of this guide to discuss. Likewise, legal claims under Section 1981 or Section 1983 do not fall under these caps because these caps are specific to Title VII and Maryland's equivalent law.

Finally, employees seeking redress for discrimination and retaliation under Title VII and its Maryland counterpart can seek lost wages and legal expenses without facing these statutory caps.

CONCLUSION

Federal and Maryland law protects various specific categories of people both from discrimination and from retaliation for the protected activity of advancing these same rights. If you believe you are being unlawfully discriminated or retaliated against, you should consult with legal counsel or governmental enforcement agencies to better understand your rights and how to enforce them.

CHAPTER ELEVEN

FEDERAL RIGHT TO RELIGIOUS ACCOMMODATION AT WORK

In addition to the other aforementioned rights that Title VII of the federal Civil Rights Act of 1964 provides, it also provides employees with bona fide religious beliefs a right to request religious accommodation at work. Religious accommodation is a reasonable adjustment to the work environment that enables employees to practice their religion while maintaining their livelihood. Some examples of religious accommodation requests include requests to wear a specific garment for bona fide religious need, to practice the Sabbath on Saturday or Sunday and never be scheduled to work on that Sabbath day, or to take time off to worship on specific religious holiday or for specific religious meetings. Whether an employer is legally required to grant the accommodation, however, depends on whether the request is reasonable or imposes an undue hardship upon the business. And again, Title VII applies only to employers with fifteen or more employees over at least twenty weeks of the year.

EXERCISING YOUR RIGHT TO RELIGIOUS ACCOMMODATION

To exercise your right to religious accommodation, you need to meet the following requirements:

1. Have a bona fide religious belief that you practice.

2. Notify the employer.

3. Make a reasonable request.

See Chalmers v. Tulon Co. of Richmond, 101 F.3d 1012, 1018 (4th Cir. 1996).

A denial of a reasonable religious accommodation request is illegal. It also can result in further religious discrimination if the denial proceeds to include discipline, such as demotion, suspension, and/or termination. If, for example, an employee's reasonable religious accommodation request is denied, but the employee takes the requested day/time off anyway and the employer then disciplines him or her in some way, that discipline can be deemed religious discrimination (see EEOC v. Firestone Fibers & Textiles Co., 515 F.3d 307, 312 (4th Cir. 2008), citing Chalmers v. Tulon Co. of Richmond, 101 F.3d 1012, 1019 (4th Cir. 1996)).

The key issue in such a situation is whether the employee can make a reasonable request that does not cause an undue burden on the business. This is because, practically speaking, providing an accommodation may either actually create an undue burden on an employer and/or an employer may believe the request is unduly burdensome. While an employer's belief may or may not meet the legal requirement to deny accommodation, if the matter ever comes before a court, it will be reduced to its facts. Religious requests require the

RELIGIOUS REQUESTS REQUIRE THE SAME REASONABLE APPROACH AS DO REQUESTS FOR REASONABLE ACCOMMODATION.

same reasonable approach as do requests for reasonable accommodation discussed in chapter 9.

The reality, therefore, is that requesting an accommodation involves some give and take between you and your employer. For instance, if you want to request certain days off, try to give the employer significant advance notice. Or, if you want to request a certain time off, you might ask the employer if taking the entire day off would be easier from an administrative perspective. If you need to pray at work for ten minutes at 10:45 a.m., for instance, this may be easier to accommodate in an office environment where you work at your own pace than in a production-oriented factory where the machines run and people work them except during the general breaks. Lastly, if your religious requirements are strict (for example, if you need to take every Friday off) but your job is incompatible with them, it might be prudent to enquire if there are other job vacancies that might better accommodate your religious need, your need for employment, and your employer's needs. For instance in a driving job, a "route" driver might need to work Monday through Friday, while the backup drivers may have more flexible schedules five to seven days per week.

Such a problem-solving approach to requesting accommodation is always preferable to a legal dispute, which can take years to resolve, may require you to bear legal expenses, and which may depend on facts about what is reasonable or an undue hardship that will not be revealed until later in the legal process. If, however, the request cannot be resolved at work, the first legally required step of enforcement is to file a charge of religious discrimination, an administrative process discussed in chapter 10.

CONCLUSION

People with bona fide religious beliefs have a right to be reasonably accommodated at work where Title VII applies. Research and know your legal rights.

CHAPTER TWELVE

EMPLOYMENT CONTRACTS AND TYPICAL CLAUSES

A good first step of any legal analysis of your rights begins with an examination of your employment contract, if you have one.

As discussed in chapter 4, a union contract is a form of employment contract, a collective one governed by federal law. An individual employment contract usually is an additional protection to the state or federal rights already covered in this guide, and often covers core terms, duties, and benefits of an employment for each side. Many aspects of an employment contract are governed by Maryland's common law of contracts in addition to any relevant employment laws.

Generally speaking, employment contracts are written. Under Maryland common law, oral agreements can constitute legal contracts. However, in the context of the presumption of at-will employment discussed in the first chapter, it will be difficult at best to establish the existence of an oral contract of employment if denied by one side, either the employee or employer.

IF YOU HAVE AN EMPLOYMENT CONTRACT THAT YOU THINK IS BEING VIOLATED, THE FIRST STEP WILL BE TO LOOK TO THE ACTUAL CONTRACTUAL PROVISION AT ISSUE.

If you have an employment contract that you think is being violated, the first step will be to look to the actual contractual provision at issue. Second, legal advice is advised. This is because each contract is specific to each work situation and how any contractual provision is written.

While addressing specific employment contracts is beyond the scope of this guide, employment contracts in general typically deal with some of the following provisions:

- pay

- benefits

- notice provisions (for quitting, being laid off, or for letting a contract renew)

- term of time (one year, nine months, etc.)

- confidentiality

- noncompete within the field of the employer's business

- nonsolicitation of the employer's workforce if you leave

- intellectual property rights

- arbitration and other dispute resolution requirements

Let's look at some of these provisions and what they do a little more closely:

- A confidentiality provision ensures the confidentiality of an employer's trade secrets, client information, and/or unique work processes.

- A noncompete provision restricts where you can work during employment or for some reasonable period of time afterward, in terms of time, geography, and industry.

- A non-solicitation provision states that if you work somewhere in competition with your employer and/or former employer, you cannot recruit and/or solicit coworkers and/or customers to join you and lasts for a reasonable period of time, during employment and often from six months to one year afterward.

- An intellectual property provision stipulates that on-the-job inventions are the employer's property and may require disclosure of any off-site inventions.

To be lawful, many of these provisions must be reasonably related to the employer's actual business and limited to accomplish legitimate commercial ends without unduly fettering someone's career. What is reasonable cannot be covered in this guide. However, Maryland case law has numerous precedents detailing how and in what circumstances these provisions have or have not been considered reasonable.

A noncompete provision of one year, for instance, is common in Maryland. In fact, if justifiable, that term could be even longer, up to two or three years, for most likely highly specialized employees and industries and due to special circumstances. Further, since Oct. 1, 2019, Maryland has outlawed noncompete agreements for any employee making $15 or less per hour, or a total of $31,200 annually or less (see Md. Code, Lab. & Empl. § 3-716(a) (2021)). This law trumps any contractual provision to the contrary and voids it.

Further, noncompete provisions cannot be too broad in geographical scope and must be factually related to the employer's actual business need. If a Baltimore County dental practice with a local clientele, for instance, imposes a noncompete provision statewide for six months after the end of employment upon a dental assistant making $21 an hour, a court might render it overbroad and so void. Hypothetically speaking, that noncompete should have been limited to Baltimore County at most, or even limited to specific mileage circumference around the business, because the practice is a general-service, local one and not a specialty with a wider clientele.

Intellectual property provisions are often utilized in the fields of science, engineering, design, research and development, invention, and the like, in which employers seek to protect their intellectual property. Such employers may, for instance, require that all inventions created on-site automatically become the property of the employer. Further, they may require that inventors in their employ disclose any side projects, weekend work, other engagements, and/or other interests in advance to prevent ownership confusion. In such situations, legal advice is highly advisable.

Employment contracts can cover various topics, such as notice requirements and term of employment. These subjects have been addressed in chapter 1. They need not be addressed again. Some employment contracts promise a payout upon termination, sometimes called a "severance." Union contracts are handled in chapters 4-5 and need not be further addressed here. An employee handbook, discussed in chapter 2, typically does not constitute a contractual promise, but is more like an employer's written guide to how it prefers to act. Written employment contracts can cover these same subjects and thus make them contractually binding.

Finally, with regard to arbitration provisions, the US Federal Arbitration Act, 9 U.S.C. § 1 et seq. (2021), encourages the imposition of arbitration upon various, but not all, kinds of employment disputes. If you seek to go to court or file a complaint with the government but you face an arbitration provision first, you should seek legal advice about your options and how to handle the arbitration requirement.

CONCLUSION

This chapter provides an overview of typical provisions in employment contracts. However, if you have contractual concerns, you should seek a professional review and legal advice. This is because employment contracts involve both the law of contracts and employment. Further, the contract language as written needs to be evaluated on a case-by-case basis.

IF YOU HAVE CONTRACTUAL CONCERNS, YOU SHOULD SEEK A PROFESSIONAL REVIEW AND LEGAL ADVICE.

CHAPTER THIRTEEN

MARYLAND COMMON LAW

"Wrongful Discharge"

T he Maryland common law claim of "wrongful discharge" is not broadly applicable. Rather, this court-created doctrine was fashioned to help employees who have been fired for advancing a clear mandate of public policy or exercising a clearly related legal right. Because this claim proceeds under Maryland's common law, the statute of limitations to file any lawsuit runs three years from the date of alleged wrongful termination or discharge. Maryland's Court of Appeals defines wrongful discharge as being comprised of the following three primary elements:

- "the employee must be discharged;

- the basis for the employee's discharge must violate some clear mandate of public policy;

- and there must be a nexus between the employee's conduct and the employer's decision to fire the employee."

Yuan v. Johns Hopkins Univ., 452 Md. 436, 451, 157 A.3d 254, 262 (2017), quoting Wholey v. Sears Roebuck, 370 Md. 38, 50-51, 803 A.2d 482, 489 (2002).

Additionally, the claim of wrongful termination or discharge has two other important requirements along with the primary elements listed above:

- There must be no other statutory civil remedy with which to seek redress, such as Title VII of the Civil Rights Act of 1964, the FMLA, or ADA, discussed in Chapters 8-10, or other specific remedy at law.

- The same "clear mandate of public policy" must be well-defined, especially by civil or criminal law.

It is optimal to have an exact citation to a specific law being advanced or enforced by the employee over which that person was fired. For instance, it is illegal to fire someone because they filed a workers' compensation claim under Md. Code, Lab. & Empl. § 9-1105 (2021), which is discussed in chapter 7, and so would justify a wrongful termination claim.

The Maryland Court of Appeals has recognized several examples to date that constitute wrongful discharge claims, including:

- demanding an employee engage in an illegal act as defined by the state or federal criminal law and then firing them for not doing so;

- firing someone who has an affirmative duty to act, such as a teacher who has an affirmative legal duty to report child abuse; and

- firing an employee who exercises the legal right to take action in court against a coworker who assaulted them.

See Yuan, 452 Md. at 459-62. The Court of Appeals further provides some interpretative flexibility when it states that the public policy "should be reasonably discernible from prescribed constitutional or statutory mandates" (see Wholey, 370 Md. at 52-54).

Let's look more closely at two examples. In the Yuan case, the Court of Appeals rejected an employee's claim of being fired for illegal "wrongful discharge," because even though he worked at Johns Hopkins University and said that he had been fired for opposing various scientific and academic research violations, there was no clear mandate of public policy in Maryland concerning research malfeasance and disputes. In so ruling, the court looked in particular to one prior precedent, which held that federal prescription labeling regulations (so highly important to the drug marketplace and safety) also did not state a clear mandate of statewide public policy in Maryland and so could not support this common law claim for wrongful discharge (see 452 Md. at 454-455). In

> IN SUM, WRONGFUL DISCHARGE IS A HIGHLY SPECIFIC LEGAL CLAIM. IT PROTECTS PEOPLE ENFORCING MARYLAND LAW IN THEIR DAILY LIVES. HOWEVER, IT IS NOT A PANACEA TO THE WORLD'S ILLS OR A SWORD TO COMBAT GENERAL UNFAIRNESS.

sum, wrongful discharge is a highly specific legal claim. It protects people enforcing Maryland law in their daily lives. However, it is not a panacea to the world's ills or a sword to combat general unfairness.

CONCLUSION

Maryland courts have held that Maryland employees fired for exercising or advancing rights protected by Maryland criminal, Maryland civil, Constitutional, and federal criminal law can state a claim for wrongful discharge, especially in specific examples upheld by the courts. Despite the claim's broad phrasing, pursing this highly focused legal claim requires the help of a legal professional.

CHAPTER FOURTEEN

THE EMPLOYEE'S DUTY TO MITIGATE DAMAGES

The law requires that employees who lose income as the result of an employer's illegal act look for work and "mitigate their damages" if they intend to seek that lost income as an award against an employer. This doctrine of "mitigation of damages" appears across various laws and statutes under the common law active in state and federal courts.

Lost income can be divided into "back pay" and "front pay," as well as other lost income categories, such as lost benefits. Back pay covers the income lost from the time of the illegal act to any final resolution, such as a settlement or court's judgment. Front pay, or future lost income, involves reasonably certain future lost earnings due to an employer's illegal act. Front pay is appropriate, for instance, where someone's career has been derailed.

When seeking owed income, an employee has a duty to seek other employment or income so as to reduce loss during this "loss" period of time. If the employee does not mitigate damages in this way, the court may hold that (barring some special circumstance) the employer is no longer responsible for covering the loss, because the employee did not seek new work.

> **WHEN SEEKING OWED INCOME, AN EMPLOYEE HAS A DUTY TO SEEK OTHER EMPLOYMENT OR INCOME SO AS TO REDUCE LOSS DURING THIS "LOSS" PERIOD OF TIME.**

This doctrine applies only to claims of lost income. Employees who fail to mitigate damages may still be permitted to collect other kinds of damages, including for emotional distress or punitive damages or legal fees incurred to redress the illegal wrong. It is, however, usually difficult to prove entitlement to emotional damages from a workplace event without medical evidence of the distress and its correlation to the workplace.

Consequently, if you have been fired illegally and you seek lost income, you should apply for at least one to two jobs per week and record the details of your search, such as the date, job title, company name, manner of application, and result. Further, you should save any receipts or other records that prove your efforts, such as emails, cover letters, and applications.

An easy way to record an employment search is in a chart. Here's a sample:

DATE APPLIED	EMPLOYER NAME AND ADDRESS	HOW APPLIED: MAIL, CALL, IN PERSON, ETC.	POSITION APPLIED FOR:	RESULTS?

UNEMPLOYMENT BENEFIT INCOME SHOULD NOT OFFSET OWED WAGES FOR LOST INCOME

Many federal courts recognize that getting unemployment benefits should not reduce an employer's liability for lost wages damages because this would enable the employer, if and when acting illegally, to rely on public benefits so as to reduce their exposure and obligation (see Reed v. Dep't of Corr., Civ. No. 7:13-CV-00543, 2014 US Dist. LEXIS 157822, at *5-6 (W.D. Va. Nov. 7, 2014); Johnson v. Ryder Truck Lines, Inc., Civ. No. 73-3., 1980 US Dist. LEXIS 13611, at *89 (W.D.N.C. Aug. 8, 1980—"Unemployment compensation, which was received by some of the plaintiffs during their back pay periods, should not be utilized to reduce back pay awards. Unemployment benefits are derived from a collateral source independent of earnings," citing NLRB v. Moss Planing Mill Co., 224 F.2d 702 (4th Cir. 1955)). Some judges, however, may disagree as applied to the specific circumstances at hand.

CONCLUSION

If you are seeking lost income due to an employer's illegal action, you have an affirmative duty to look for work, find work when possible, and so mitigate your damages. Otherwise, you face being denied lost income at a court. So, keep track of it. Remember, knowledge is power. Know your rights.

CHAPTER FIFTEEN

GATHERING AND PRESERVING EVIDENCE

A t my law office, the first step in any legal process is a legal consultation, especially for a workplace dispute. While preparations for every employment case are specific to the situation, and the scope of a legal consultation cannot be assumed, I always consider four fundamental questions:

- What laws are involved, based on the facts presented?

- What laws can help the person's situation?

- What evidence does the person have so far?

- What are the next legal steps and also nonlegal options?

This chapter focuses on the third question, what evidence a person has for what they say, as well as how to gather and preserve that evidence. It also provides a basic overview of what constitutes relevant legal evidence but does not include the various types of evidence allowed at courts.

WHAT IS EVIDENCE AND WHAT CONSTITUTES RELEVANT EVIDENCE?

By legal definition, "evidence" means documents, witnesses, statistics, or matters of public record that are admissible at court. Further, out of all this evidence, courts, governmental agencies, and lawyers will focus on what facts are relevant to any legal claim.

Under court procedural rules, only relevant evidence is admissible evidence at court, and in this way, the courts exclude the "telephone book," so to speak, and other mere details and background. See Fed. Rule of Evidence 401 and Md. Rule of Evidence 5-401. These rules define relevant evidence as that which makes a fact more or less likely to be true. Relevant evidence is admissible under Fed. Rules 402 and Md. Rule 5-402, respectively.

What is relevant evidence? Relevant evidence is evidence that is consequential in determining the outcome of the case. If, for example, an employer fires an employee for alleged poor performance and the fired employee claims the termination was discriminatory (due, for instance, to his or her religion or having recently filed a workers' compensation claim), then the most relevant evidence would be that which proves or disproves discriminatory, illegal motive on the employer's part. In contrast to this hypothetical, if both parties agree the employee was fired, then that fact of termination will be established, and the evidence about motive for the termination will be preeminent.

As noted above, documents including letters, calendars, diaries, emails, text messages, employment contracts, and the employee handbook all can constitute evidence for a legal claim in an employment dispute. Further, the results of the court discovery process, discussed in the next chapter, can help employees obtain more evidence.

In terms of establishing facts before a court or government agency, the quality of evidence matters. Document-based evidence helps. If, for example, you have an email showing the date and time an incident at issue occurred or when and how a complaint about harassment was made, that email is stronger evidence of the date and time than merely your recollection if the date and time is disputed. Additionally, courts and governmental investigators deal with many people, each of whom presents things as they see them. Plus, memories can grow hazy or be faulty. Documents, on the other hand, "speak for themselves." They are, therefore, often preferred as evidence in many forums.

> **MEMORIES CAN GROW HAZY OR BE FAULTY. DOCUMENTS, ON THE OTHER HAND, "SPEAK FOR THEMSELVES."**

GATHERING AND PRESERVING EVIDENCE

The following tips will help you to gather and preserve written evidence that will strengthen your case in court should you need to bring one against your employer.

Send an Email

There are many ways to preserve evidence in written form. For instance, if you verbally ask your supervisor for FMLA leave and your supervisor grants it, send a polite, confirmatory email, such as the following:

DEAR FRANK,

THANK YOU SO MUCH FOR LETTING ME KNOW EARLIER TODAY THAT THE FMLA LEAVE I REQUESTED SHOULD BE NO PROBLEM. I APPRECIATE IT. I WILL BE CONTACTING HR FOR THE FORMS. THANKS AGAIN.

Such a confirmatory email serves several purposes. It documents your verbal communication. Second, it contributes to a good relationship between you and your employer, as everyone likes to be thanked. Third, it is polite and well written. Consequently, should it be necessary to present as evidence, it will make a positive impression upon the decision-maker as to your professionalism and temperament. Do remember to print it out or keep a copy. If fired, you will lose immediate access to any work-based email accounts and emails there.

Document Complaints in Writing

You may make discrimination or retaliation complaints orally; however, if you do, you need to document the complaint in writing. You could do so in a polite confirmatory email that proves the employer understands the issue involved and discussed it with you, as shown in the example above.

Alternatively, let's assume you make a discrimination complaint via calling "1-800 hotline" or via an electronic portal and you cannot make a copy of it. You also can record the details of your complaint in a dated diary entry, made as contemporaneously as possible. If using a hotline, you can ask for any confirmation code for having received your phone call.

Take a Picture

If you are facing retaliatory threats in the form of graffiti, for instance, take a picture of it.

Keep Copies

If you state something to your employer in a letter, make and keep a copy.

Consider a Fax Machine

If you are submitting evidence, a complaint, or a request to an employer or government agency—such as a doctor's note, discrimination/retaliation complaint, or FMLA paperwork—using a fax machine is a great way to preserve evidence. Why? First, you keep what you send. The fax makes the transmitted copy. Second, fax machines provide delivery confirmation. In the same way, email and certified US mail both create transmission receipts.

Calendars and Diaries

Do not overlook calendars and diaries, which are useful tools for any matter lasting several weeks or more—for instance, in illegal harassment cases or working without full pay. If you keep a calendar or diary, noting, for instance, work performed and wages owed, the record will be clear weeks, months, or years later.

The purpose of making any calendar or diary entry as close to the event described as possible has to do with helping that document be admissible in a court of law. It helps.

File a Police Report

If you are physically attacked at work or very clearly threatened with physical assault, or your car is mysteriously damaged at work, you can file a police report.

Keep Your Evidence in a Safe, Off-Worksite Place

If you have a significant workplace problem and the employer is behaving illegally, remember that if you are fired, you will have no legal right to access your workplace email account (or anything else at your work desk) until a lawsuit is filed and the court "discovery" process begins. So make sure to keep your evidence in a safe, off-worksite place.

Be Mindful of Your Lack of Privacy at Work

While this may appear to be common sense, an employee facing a workplace problem should remember that emails and documents on an employer's computer and email system are the property of the employer. So any assumption of their privacy will be false. If, for instance, you keep notes on a small pad and put it in the glove box of a work vehicle, it might be confiscated or cleaned out and thrown away.

The employer has a private property right over their workplace and equipment and a right to possess or inspect any communication created with work tools. This includes any correspondence with your own attorney if you wrote it on or sent it via a work email account. Consequently, write any legal correspondence of your own on your personal laptop or phone and via your own private email account.

WHAT TYPES OF EVIDENCE ARE ADMISSIBLE IN COURT?

It is advisable to consult a lawyer with regard to what types of evidence will be admissible in court, as this guide covers the admissibility of basic evidence only, not the full range of possible evidence for any specific case. Further, as noted in chapter 6 concerning unemployment benefits, proving something before an administrative agency does not necessarily involve the court rules of evidence, and so the presentation should be tailored accordingly.

In Maryland, documents such as those listed in the tips section above may be admissible under the doctrines of recorded recollection and/or present sense impression (see Md. Rule 5-802.1(e); Md. Rule 803(b)(1)). While the latter often only applies to near contemporaneous written accounts, the conundrum of being an employee on the job should permit some leeway.

Employee records of time worked are routinely considered in owed overtime and owed pay disputes where the employer denies it and yet fails to keep accurate records (see e.g., Marroquin v. Canales, 505 F. Supp. 2d 283 (D. Md. 2007)). Self-kept records can be rebutted, but they at least provide a reasonable basis upon which to seek owed wages (*id.* at 295-298).

Practice Diplomacy

When gathering and preserving evidence, don't forget to practice diplomacy. It is better to take a problem-solving approach to resolving a workplace issue, especially before the matter has escalated.

> **WHEN GATHERING AND PRESERVING EVIDENCE, DON'T FORGET TO PRACTICE DIPLOMACY.**

CONCLUSION

In the process of deciding employment disputes, government investigators and/or courts of law look first to the evidence of what happened. Therefore, gathering and preserving evidence is a crucial part of any legal claim.

At court, the discovery process can help you obtain further evidence, and this is discussed in the next chapter.

CHAPTER SIXTEEN

USING DISCOVERY AT COURT

T he legal process of discovery in a court of law permits one party to obtain evidence from the other as well as establish and develop relevant evidence. Both Maryland state and federal courts provide for discovery, which becomes available through the filing of a lawsuit. The discovery process, beginning at Federal Rule of Civil Procedure 26 for US District Courts and Maryland Rules of Civil Procedure 2-401 for Maryland Circuit Courts, permits one party to obtain evidence from the other in the following basic forms:

a. documents ("Requests for Production of Documents")

b. answers to specific questions ("Answers to Interrogatories")

c. depositions of people before a court reporter under oath

d. responses to "Requests for Admissions"

e. inspection of premises, if applicable

f. examinations of someone's mental health and status, if applicable, for specific good cause shown

g. other forms of reasonable discovery, including expert reports, expert evaluations, expert witnesses, the appropriate use of public records, relevant online evidence, and so on

Employers control the workplace, so in employment cases, discovery often is a large part of litigation to advance employee rights, to obtain evidence still at work. However, court discovery does not permit a fishing expedition. Discovery is not permitted to be a form of expensive harassment, or what one court called "overdiscovery" (see, e.g., Mancia v. Mayflower Textile Servs. Co., 253 F.R.D. 354 (D. Md. 2008)).

Rather, discovery must be focused on relevant, admissible evidence and its likely sources (see *id.*)

If you have an attorney, that attorney likely will use some or all of the discovery devices listed above.

If you are representing yourself, however, you should research discovery tools and know, at least, the discovery devices listed at letters a-b above: (a) "Requests for Production of Documents" and (b) "Answers to Interrogatories." These are basic, helpful tools of written discovery.

COURT DISCOVERY DOES NOT PERMIT A FISHING EXPEDITION. DISCOVERY IS NOT PERMITTED TO BE A FORM OF EXPENSIVE HARASSMENT.

If you are involved in a lawsuit, you yourself may need to answer discovery, including gathering documents and answering "Interrogatories."

This guide cannot provide extensive guidance on court discovery. However, some generally useful tips for employees are as follows on the next page.

MARYLAND CIRCUIT COURT FORM INTERROGATORIES AS OF 2021

STANDARD GENERAL INTERROGATORY NO. 1:

Identify each person (other than a person intended to be called as an expert witness at trial) having discoverable information that tends to support a position that you have taken or intend to take in this action, including any claim for damages, and state the subject matter of the information possessed by that person.

STANDARD GENERAL INTERROGATORY NO. 2:

Identify each person whom you expect to call as an expert witness at trial, state the subject matter on which the expert is expected to testify, state the substance of the findings and opinions to which the expert is expected to testify and a summary of the grounds for each opinion, and, with respect to an expert whose findings and opinions were acquired in anticipation of litigation or for trial, summarize the qualifications of the expert, state the terms of the expert's compensation, and attach to your answers any available list of publications written by the expert and any written report made by the expert concerning the expert's findings and opinions.

STANDARD GENERAL INTERROGATORY NO. 3:

If you intend to rely upon any documents, electronically stored information, or tangible things to support a position that you have taken or intend to take in the action, including any claim for damages, provide a brief description, by category and location, of all such documents, electronically stored information, and tangible things, and identify all persons having possession, custody, or control of them.

STANDARD GENERAL INTERROGATORY NO. 5:

If any person carrying on an insurance business might be liable to satisfy part or all of a judgment that might be entered in this action or to indemnify or reimburse for payments made to satisfy the judgment, identify that person, state the applicable policy limits of any insurance agreement under which the person might be liable, and describe any question or challenge raised by the person relating to coverage for this action.

Source: Maryland Rules, Title II Appendix ("Civil Procedure—Circuit Court"), Form No. 3. General Interrogatories (2021)

The above sample Interrogatories Nos. 1-3 and No. 5 are those that an employee might use. You should expect to be asked the same thing. Plus, you most certainly will be asked some form of this one: "Itemize and show how you calculate any economic damages claimed by you in this action, and describe any noneconomic damages claimed" (Standard General Interrogatory No. 4).

The Local Rules for our US District Court also has some form discovery as well as guidance on discovery procedure. Here are samples from the federal template Request for Production of Documents:

- all documents referred to in your Answers to Interrogatories

- all contracts and agreements entered between plaintiff and defendant concerning the occurrence or transaction

Here are some that I might use, from my practice, as well as use as templates to be revised to apply to any case at hand:

- the employee handbook in effect during the facts stated in plaintiff's complaint

- any employer policy document upon which the employer relies to support the employer's legal and/or factual defense

- any documents supporting a denial and/or affirmative defense in defendant's answer

- any document evidencing a denial and/or affirmative defense in defendant's answer

- all documents and communications to and from the defendant and the EEOC and/or MCCR or any equivalent local agency, including but not limited to emails, letters, briefings, correspondence, attachments to emails, position statements, charges, rebuttals, exhibits, and the like, and including any documents made by third parties that are transmitted among these responsive documents and communications

- all documents that defendant intends to introduce into evidence and/or use at trial with a witness or otherwise

- personnel file of plaintiff, including copies of the front and back covers, and including regardless of how defendant titles it and/or separates it into separate "files," any annual performance reviews, performance reviews, workplace awards, evaluations, and the like; any employment application, reference checks, initial interview notes with plaintiff and/or with references, credit and/or background reports, and including all documents concerning plaintiff's workplace performance, such as performance reviews, disciplinary documents, PIPs, written counseling, notes about oral counseling, memos, emails, awards, notes, and the like

CONCLUSION

This chapter provides a rudimentary overview of discovery so as to help you understand its basic framework. However, the samples above are not guaranteed to be suitable for your particular case. In my practice, I tailor my discovery for each case. So consider these samples solely as general templates. If you intend to file a lawsuit, representation or legal advice is advisable, especially in terms of handling the court discovery process.

CHAPTER SEVENTEEN

HIRING A LAWYER

When hiring a lawyer to handle an employment matter, it is advisable to seek an employment attorney with experience in negotiating a broad array of workplace and termination-related disputes.

A legal consultation is a good first step in this process. In fact, in my own law practice, I require a consultation so potential clients are informed when making choices about whether, how, and when to proceed with legal action.

Knowing what your options are with regard to these choices both empowers your judgment and brings peace of mind. Second, a consultation will give you a sense of the lawyer's personality and experience, helping you to decide whether he or she is a good fit for you. While a consultation, or even several consultations with different lawyers, might seem costly, it may help you save money down the road. Legal disputes can be expensive. I have handled complex discrimination matters that took two to four years to resolve. Even those that resolve "sooner," so to speak, often take six months to a year. So the cost of a legal consultation or two in order to educate yourself before making decisions is prudent.

WHILE A CONSULTATION, OR EVEN SEVERAL CONSULTATIONS WITH DIFFERENT LAWYERS, MIGHT SEEM COSTLY, IT MAY HELP YOU SAVE MONEY DOWN THE ROAD.

There are some niche areas within the broader arena of employment law that you should know about. Union-related employment law, for example, comprises its own vast body of law and regulation. Lawyers who focus on union-related disputes and workplaces sometimes are called labor lawyers. Similarly, workers' compensation is a highly regulated niche of employment law with highly specific processes and forms. Consequently, there are lawyers and law firms that focus on this workers' comp [or compensation] field.

How do you tell if someone has in-depth experience in employment law? First, you can ask. Second, you can read their website or other business information. Third, many employment attorneys are barred in state and federal courts because of the plethora of federal laws regulating employment. A federal court appearance requires a separate admissions process and is a sign of an experienced employment counsel who practices in both state and federal court.

HOW TO PREPARE FOR YOUR LEGAL CONSULTATION

The legal consultation process, again, is a preliminary step. It can help you ensure you have found the right lawyer and, most importantly, know your legal as well as nonlegal options.

Your legal consultation will require you to keep an open mind. This is because there may be a variety of ways to approach the resolution of your problem.

Before you arrive at your legal consultation, you might consider these questions:

- Would it be helpful to write down questions in advance to better keep track of them?

- Do you have in hand, printed out, any important documents to be reviewed? If not, can you bring them?

- Are there important emails, texts, or other communications that can be printed out or copied for your case so the lawyer can see (versus simply hear about) them?

- Are there important witnesses who can speak in your favor, and do you have their names, phone numbers, and/or other contact information handy?

- What questions do you have about your options, or best next steps?

- What is your goal?

- What are the legal and/or nonlegal options to achieve your goal(s)?

- Of any legal options presented, what are the possible outcomes?

- Of any legal options presented, what might be the expenses or consequences?

CONCLUSION

Remember, knowledge is power, so know your rights.

CHAPTER EIGHTEEN

BEING ENTREPRENEURIAL

T he world we live in is changing rapidly, due in no small part to the rise of multiple technologies, instantaneous communication systems, and increasing populations. This is true if we compare ourselves to either a century ago or a few decades ago, that is, to the year 1900 or even the year 2000.

The internet, social media, smart phones, artificial intelligence, robotics, and increasing automation, for example, all have changed our lives and work significantly in the last thirty years alone. Some might compare the computer revolution, which began in the mid-twentieth century, to the Industrial Revolution, which began in the eighteenth. Such a comparison would be apt, given that the computer revolution has replaced many manual and mechanical processes, enables us to store and process vast quantities of information, and to communicate digitally. The Industrial Revolution replaced home- and handmade goods with mass production, and the computer revolution has or is replacing many physical goods and related travel and transportation requirements, among other aspects of life that existed even a few decades ago.

AS A TWENTY-FIRST CENTURY EMPLOYEE, IF YOU WANT NOT ONLY TO SURVIVE BUT ALSO THRIVE, YOU NEED TO BE SAVVY AND ENTREPRENEURIAL.

Further, there are simply more people today than ever before. In 1900, there were around 1.6 billion people on Earth, as compared with close to eight billion today, a figure that continues to grow. Therefore, as a twenty-first-century employee, if you want not only to survive but also thrive, you need to be savvy and entrepreneurial.

Countries with the largest population in 1950

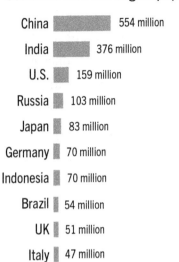

Country	Population
China	554 million
India	376 million
U.S.	159 million
Russia	103 million
Japan	83 million
Germany	70 million
Indonesia	70 million
Brazil	54 million
UK	51 million
Italy	47 million

Countries with the largest population in 2020

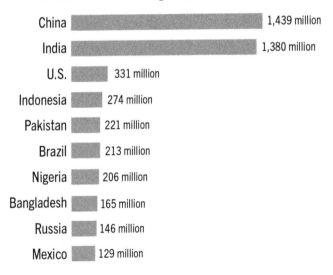

Country	Population
China	1,439 million
India	1,380 million
U.S.	331 million
Indonesia	274 million
Pakistan	221 million
Brazil	213 million
Nigeria	206 million
Bangladesh	165 million
Russia	146 million
Mexico	129 million

Population Growth
Source: Pew Research

I use the terms "savvy" and "entrepreneurial" for good reason. When I was entering young adulthood in the 1990s, a much-discussed topic of conversation was that the era of employment with one company for the duration of one's working life had passed. A cultural norm about two generations back from my own, the idea that a person could rise up the career ladder, then retire from the same firm with which he or she had begun was already fading, and since then has become near obsolete.

Instead, rather than referring to ascension through the ranks of just one company, the term "career" increasingly means a path upon which you can accrue ever more specialized skills, talents, and knowledge with which to become better equipped to navigate the marketplace. The more skills, talents, and knowledge acquired, the greater your agency. This resource might include a network of allies, current and past business colleagues, former employers with whom you have good relations, and a variety of acquaintances.

Acquiring the credentials to practice a profession—be it in the field of education, medicine, law, or in the trades, as, for example, a teacher, physician's assistant, doctor, lawyer, electrician, or plumber—also helps insulate you from the myriad changes of our times. This is because, as a professional, you are required to keep up with developments in your field by reading industry publications, networking, and collaborating with colleagues who also are preparing themselves for and experiencing change. In the same vein, instead of working for just one employer, for example, you might start a business at the same time. This advice is less advice than observation of what people are doing today.

The legal rights that we have as employees are changing too. As noted in chapter 10, for instance, Maryland law in 2019 expanded the scope of statewide harassment law to any employer with one or more employees. And, as noted in chapter 12, Maryland recently banned noncompete agreements for any employee making $15 per hour or less. These laws, among others, will continue to evolve.

Therefore, not only is it crucial to be as knowledgeable as possible about your legal rights, it's also important to understand how technological changes affect everyone so as to best navigate the workplace today. As Daniel Goleman posits in *Emotional Intelligence: Why It Can Matter More Than IQ* (2005), it is essential to cultivate emotional skills to navigate one's career and workplace success. This is true at any time—and especially in these changing times.

As Andrew Yang points out in *The War on Normal People: The Truth About America's Disappearing Jobs and Why Universal Basic Income Is Our Future* (2019), computers, robotics, automation, and technology are replacing many jobs once thought to be bedrocks. While Mr. Yang, a former tech entrepreneur, identifies himself as a Democrat, his view isn't party line. Rather, it is based on his business experience, and his proposed solutions are still considered unconventional. Nebraska Republican Senator Ben Sasse raises similar concerns about how technological automation reduces work, in addition to raising alarms about the cultural impact of our technological dependence, in *The Vanishing American Adult: Our Coming-of-Age Crisis—and How to Rebuild a Culture of Self-Reliance* (2017). Being educated about what is happening all around us is crucial to one's career.

The effect of social media alone on the employment arena is changing the very way that people perceive and act in the workplace (not to mention in other arenas too). Author Newton Lee, in *Facebook Nation: Total Information Awareness* (2013), for instance, argues that using Facebook makes people more self-centered. Because this trait bears on how we deal with relationships at work, whether with coworkers, supervisors, or customers, it is especially important to be aware of developments like this and to hone the emotional skills necessary to deal with it. The technologies that people use affect how they act and think. Consequently, our gadgets and devices also have an impact on how businesses market to customers and how professionals interact with the clients to whom they provide services.

CONCLUSION

Today, we live in a mobile, digital culture in which technology has vastly increased the speed and complexity with which we work. This will continue to necessitate the evolution of employment law, and the twenty-first century workplace will continue to evolve too. Therefore, whether self-employed or an employee, you need both a creative, entrepreneurial spirit and a savvy, informed perspective to survive and thrive.

KNOWLEDGE IS POWER, AND PREPARATION IS WISE.

Remember, knowledge is power, and preparation is wise.

FURTHER RESOURCES

This guide does not provide legal advice. Legal advice is specific to each workplace and each person's unique situation. Further, the guide provides only an overview of major, but not all, employee rights. For instance, whistleblower protections, filing complaints about workplace safety, evaluating claims under Maryland contract law, dealing with civil service rules for governmental workers, and sundry other niche topics, including the range of damages available from an illegal employment act, are left out or just touched upon. However, if you wish to research more about topics within or beyond the scope of this guide, you can consult the following resources:

ONLINE GOVERNMENTAL RESOURCES

The US Equal Employment Opportunity Commission (www.eeoc.gov)

This federal agency enforces various federal employment laws, especially those federal laws discussed in chapters 8-11, and some not discussed in this guide. The EEOC publishes information about these laws and so is a useful online resource.

The Maryland Commission on Civil Rights (www.mccr.maryland.gov)

Maryland's agency dedicated to combating discrimination publishes information on Maryland discrimination and retaliation laws, such as some of the laws discussed in chapters 8-11.

Maryland's Department of Labor (www.dllr. state.md.us)

This state agency regulates many aspects of the Maryland workplace, including handling unemployment benefit claims, wage-related issues, and workplace safety.

The US Occupational Safety and Health Administration (www.osha.gov)

This agency enforces workplace safety nationally. Its whistleblower division, where you can report work hazards and safety violations, is online at www.osha. gov/whistleblower/WBComplaint.

The Family Medical Leave Act ("FMLA") at the US Dept. of Labor (www.dol.gov/agencies/ whd/fmla)

The FMLA is enforced by the US Department of Labor, which publishes various information, updates, regulations, and guidance about it online.

REFERENCE BOOKS

Maryland Employment Law by Stanley Mazaroff and Todd Horn (LexisNexis, 2nd ed., 2021) is an annually updated treatise on Maryland employment law. This reference guide provides an in-depth presentation on Maryland employment law and court precedents about it and is written by attorneys for other attorneys. So it may be a challenging read.

Every Employee's Guide to the Law by Lewin G. Joel III (Pantheon; revised 2011) offers an affordable, very readable overview of employment law in about 350 pages (although it is a little dated, as the book is ten years old). Written by a Connecticut-based lawyer, this paperback surveys the law nationally.

Labor Law for the Rank & Filer: Building Solidarity While Staying Clear of the Law by Staughton Lynd and Daniel Gross (PM Press, 2nd ed., 2011) is an affordable paperback guide to union-related laws for union members. It provides a good historical context for union workplace rights (though, being ten years old, may not cover the latest in labor law).

Pleading Causes of Action in Maryland by Paul Mark Sander and James K. Archibald (Maryland State Bar Association, 6th ed., 2018). This legal resource has an excellent opening chapter on the "Fundamental Concepts and Mechanics" of filing a lawsuit in Maryland Circuit Courts, the state's major trial courts (pp. 1-86). It also covers the small claims process (pp. 991-1017). While expensive, it can be found at most law libraries.

Discovery Problems and Their Solutions by Paul W. Grimm, Charles S. Fax, and Paul Mark Sandler (American Bar Association, 2nd. ed., 2009). This book covers discovery in a conversational though still technical format. A third edition was published in 2014.

ACKNOWLEDGMENTS

For each of my clients, it has been an honor to represent you before governments and courts in your journey toward resolution or justice.

To the University of Baltimore School of Law, which provided a generous merit scholarship, many opportunities, and a great education, all of which helped launch my legal career, thank you.

To exemplary editors Celene Adams and Josh Houston, thank you for making this guide clearer and better. To book designer Mary Hamilton, thank you for this wonderful design and cover art. To the Advantage Media production team led by Rachel Griffin, Keith Kopsack, and Tracy Hill, thank you.

Thank you to Advantage Media Group for bringing this guide to the world.

To my legal professors at the University of Baltimore School of Law: Professor Matthew Lindsay, Professor Audrey McFarlane, Professor Kim Wehle, Professor and Dean Phillip Closius, Professor and Assistant Dean Claudia Diamond, Professor Michael Hayes of Labor Law, and Adjunct Professor Michael Spekter of the Employment Law Trial Team, thank you for the inspiration, support, and your own shining light.

To the Honorable Duncan W. Keir, former chief judge of the US Bankruptcy Court for the District of Maryland, thank you for choosing me as a 2010 judicial summer intern, where I learned invaluable lessons on how to practice the law.

To the Honorable Paul W. Grimm, of the US District Court for the District of Maryland, I am honored to have been part of your evidence and discovery seminar classes and still draw from those wellsprings.

To colleagues Julius Blattner, Esq., Curtis Cooper, Esq., F. J. Collins, Esq., Paul Mark Sandler, Esq., Tom Gross, Esq., Mike Steer, Esq., Matthew Esworthy, Esq., Steve Lebau, Esq., Richard Neuworth, Esq., Jack Sturgill, Esq., Rich Lebovitz, Esq., Adam Roa,

Esq., G. Macy Nelson, Esq., and others, thank you for sharing your wisdom, collegiality, and collaborations along the way.

To Arabella and Atlas, Atlas and Arabella, with love.

ABOUT THE AUTHOR

Attorney Gregg Mosson focuses on representing employees in claims of illegal discrimination, illegal retaliation, disability rights violations, wrongful terminations, FMLA violations, employment contract disputes, severance negotiations, and when seeking owed wages. He represents family members navigating the complexities of separation, divorce, custody, and alimony. He also represents people seeking disability benefits from Social Security.

Mr. Mosson takes a mindful approach to the practice of law. He aims to provide his clients with strategic and holistic advice during the legal process. Mr. Mosson also consults with people about employment and family matters behind the scenes.

Mr. Mosson practices regularly in Maryland state and federal courts, as well as before the US Equal Employment Opportunity Commission, Maryland Commission on Civil Rights, Social Security Administration, Maryland Department of Labor, US National Labor Relations Board, and other administrative bodies.

Mr. Mosson's articles on employment law and civil procedure have appeared in the *Maryland Bar Journal* and *Trial Reporter* of Maryland, and he has published legal scholarship in the *University of Baltimore Law Review* of Maryland and *Western State University Law Review* of California. His commentary also has appeared in *The Baltimore Sun*, *The Oregonian*, and *The Futurist*. He has been named a Rising Star in Plaintiff's Employment Law by Maryland *Super Lawyers Magazine* from 2016 through 2021.

Mr. Mosson is a summa cum laude graduate of the University of Baltimore School of Law, where he served as staff editor and then associate comments editor of the *Law Review*. During the spring 2019 and 2020 semesters, he served as an adjunct professor of law at the University of Baltimore School of Law, teaching persuasive legal writing to first-year law students.

Mr. Mosson is involved in the legal community as an active member of the Baltimore County Bar Association and Maryland Association of Justice.

Printed in the USA
CPSIA information can be obtained
at www.ICGtesting.com
JSHW012028140824
68134JS00033B/2937

9 781642 253474